'Perfect plc'?

Titles available in the McGraw-Hill Developing Organizations Series

THE ORGANIZATIONAL LEARNING CYCLE
How We Can Learn Collectively
Nancy Dixon
ISBN 0-07707937-X

THE WISDOM OF STRATEGIC LEARNING
The Self Managed Learning Solution
Ian Cunningham
ISBN 0-07707894-2

DEVELOPING STRATEGIC THOUGHT
Rediscovering the Art of Direction Giving
Edited by Bob Garratt
ISBN 0-07707986-8

PERSONAL AND ORGANIZATIONAL TRANSFORMATION
The True Challenge of Continual Quality Improvement
Dalmar Fisher and William Torbert
ISBN 0-07707834-9

LEARNING AT THE TOP
Alan Mumford
ISBN 0-07709066-7

LEARNING ORGANIZATIONS IN PRACTICE
Michael Pearn, Chris Mulrooney and Keri Roderick
ISBN 0-07707744-X

CONSULTANT'S JOURNEY
A Professional and Personal Odyssey
Roger Harrison
ISBN 0-07709086-6

THE COLLECTED PAPERS OF ROGER HARRISON
Roger Harrison
ISBN 0-07709090-X

For further information on these titles and other forthcoming books please contact

The Product Manager, Professional Books, McGraw-Hill Book Company Europe, Shoppenhangers Road, Maidenhead, Berkshire SL6 2QL, United Kingdom
Telephone ++(0) 1628 23432   Fax ++(0) 1628 770224

'Perfect plc'?
The purpose and practice of organizational learning

MIKE PEDLER and KATH ASPINWALL

McGraw-Hill Book Company

London · New York · St Louis · San Francisco · Auckland
Bogotá · Caracas · Lisbon · Madrid · Mexico
Milan · Montreal · New Delhi · Panama · Paris · San Juan
São Paulo · Singapore · Sydney · Tokyo · Toronto

Published by
McGRAW-HILL Book Company Europe
Shoppenhangers Road, Maidenhead, Berkshire SL6 2QL, England
Telephone: 01628 23432
Fax: 01628 770224

British Library Cataloguing in Publication Data

Pedler, Mike
    Perfect plc?: Purpose and Practice of Organizational
Learning. – (McGraw-Hill Developing Organizations Series)
I. Title II. Aspinwall, Kath III. Series 658.407124

ISBN 0–07–709130–2

Library of Congress Cataloging-in-Publication Data

Pedler, Mike.
    Perfect plc?: the purpose and practice of organizational learning / Mike
Pedler and Kath Aspinwall.
        p. cm. – (McGraw-Hill developing organizations series) Includes
bibliographical references and index.
ISBN 0–07–709130–2 (alk. paper)
1. Organizational learning. I. Aspinwall, Kath. II. Title. III. Series.
HD58.82.P43
302.3'5–dc20

McGraw-Hill

A Division of The McGraw-Hill Companies

1234 CUP 9876

Typeset by Computape (Pickering) Ltd, North Yorkshire
and printed and bound in Great Britain at the University Press, Cambridge
Printed on permanent paper in compliance with ISO Standard 9706

Contents

Acknowledgements

We'd like to thank all the people who contributed to this book. Richard Plumb and Anthony Fretwell-Downing were the main contributors to the Fretwell Downing case in Chapter 3; to Richard go special thanks because it was his story that enabled us to break an early block in the writing.

The research on which Chapter 4 is based was carried out jointly with Ian Anderson, then Managing Director of the David Hall partnership; he contributed greatly to the ideas here. Thanks to Peter Keary (Elton Hotel), Rob Drohan, (ACE Conveyor Equipment Ltd), Ron Allock (Weldrick Group), Ian Byrne (Fencing Construction) and Ted Campbell (Gorseline) for providing extracts from the case studies on their companies.

We had help from lots of people in United Distillers for the case in Chapter 5. Chief among these were Chris Bones, Mike Pemberton, Phil Radcliff and Nancy Pile. Terry Hutton and Breck Arnzen contributed to the SmithKline Beecham case, while Rick Lent was the stimulating co-author of many of the ideas here.

Marie Lowe and her staff provided the encouraging Wisewood Primary School story in Chapter 6, and the staff of the Practice Development Unit at Seacroft Hospital, Leeds, were a true inspiration—thanks especially to Hugo Mascie-Taylor, Steve Page and Debbie Lee.

In Chapter 7, the Barnardo's case owed its origins to Susan Hayes' MSc thesis. Thanks to her and also to Mike Jarman for the development of what appears here; also to Maggie Rowlands who told us about Home-Start and Frances Hunt about Age Concern.

The Traidcraft case in Chapter 8 has its origins in contacts over several years with Richard Evans, whose mission to spread the fair trade message resonates with some of our ideas about the learning organization. Managing Director Philip Angier, his fellow directors and a frank group of managers made significant contributions. Sharon Brownfield introduced us to the idea of the balanced scorecard and provided the examples given.

In Chapter 9, thanks again to Philip Angier of Traidcraft and Chris Bones of United Distillers for their understandings of the E-Flow model; also to Dave Clarsen and the many people who contributed to the Manor Employment Project story.

Then there are all those present and past colleagues and friends who have influenced us and contributed their ideas and thoughts. There are so many of these and some of their names appear as references or in the text. Thanks particularly to the Learning Company Project collective—Tom, John, Chris and Gloria—whose ideas about the learning organization and organizational learning continue to inspire and baffle.

Finally, thanks to the anonymous Traidcraft manager who gave us such a good title for the book, and to Julia Riddlesdell, our editor, for reminding us of it.

Mike Pedler and Kath Aspinwall
Sheffield, May 1995

Introduction

Can organizations learn? And, if so, how do they do this? Furthermore, why do they want to learn—what is their purpose? And what may be the consequences of that learning.

A young manager gave us the title for our book. Her vision illustrates perfectly the urge to become better, which is the hallmark of the learning organization:

> Most people are here not just because it's a job, but because they want to be here ... they care far more about their work than they would elsewhere and they want the best from the organization. There's a sense of self-criticism and frustration in pushing themselves quite hard. What happens in Traidcraft is that there is this notional 'Perfect plc' ... we always compare ourselves with that and everyone has their own individual 'Perfect plc'.
>
> (From the Traidcraft plc case, Chapter 8)

In the best organizations, people excel *and* learn—it's part of being in that company. They recognize that there is no such thing as 'permanent excellence'; you have to *stay* excellent. The learning organization must aim to continue its learning and development if it is to achieve its purpose.

This question of purpose is critical. If we get better at learning, what is this learning for? What are the consequences of our action and our learning, and do we endorse them?

Varieties of organizational learning

The idea of the learning organization is an attractive, if elusive, vision. One problem is that no one can take you to a learning company and say this is it:

> A learning company or organization is not a defined end state. It is the journey, not the destination. As Carl Rogers put it 'we are all in a process of becoming'. Hence, organizations that embrace learning commit to an ongoing process. It would be a contra-

diction in terms to say 'We are now a learning organization—we've got the plaque on the wall—what's our next project?'
(Hughes, 1995)

Fortunately, however, organizational learning can be an everyday event. Processes of learning, beyond the individual and in the context of a whole company, are matters of vital interest for companies aiming to survive, develop and be fit for the future. Like people, all organizations learn—and sometimes fail to learn. What do these learning processes look like? How can they be improved? How do they vary from one company to another? This book surveys a variety of organizational settings in an attempt to answer these questions.

The word *company* is used for any group of people engaged in joint enterprise. It captures the essence of organizations as *learning communities* better than the more mechanical *organization*. However much we would like to reclaim the old meaning of company in this way, the fact is that the commercial connotations of the word are so strong that it sometimes simply does not work—for example with voluntary and public service organizations. The compromise is to use both words, but to favour 'company' when we can.

A variety of learning organizations

Tom Lloyd starts his book *The 'Nice' Company* with the proposition that companies are an 'intelligent, non-human species' at an early stage of their development. Two contemporary forces make this an interesting perspective. First, in times of rapid and accelerating change, companies are formed, mature, decline, merge and disappear with increasing speed. This visible lifecycle in things that formerly seemed permanent and unchanging, brings into play a second force—the use of the 'organic' lens through which to see 'the organization'—the company being seen as an organism, as a living, developing, ageing being. This looks quite different to Weber's impersonal, machine-like, bureaucratic ideal that has been a dominant metaphor for many years.

Supposing that organizations *can* be seen as a species—developing and proliferating in wide variety—like people, they have unique characteristics; no one exactly reproduces another. Their origins, products, processes, life stages, markets or contexts combine to produce hundreds of thousands of individual entities. The differences between an owner-managed manufacturer employing 50 people and the million strong UK National Health Service, or between the 9-year-old global software house and the 200-year-old local firm of solicitors are arguably more obvious than their similarities.

There is also great variety in the forms that managing, organizing and learning take in companies. Generic models can only embrace this variety—in big and small, private and public, commercial or human service companies—at the cost of much loss of focus. Although companies, as members of the same species, do share a common heritage of ideas and methods about how to produce things and manage people, it's the doing that is difficult. Though the script of management may be written, it's the performance that counts. Managing is a performing art.

Companies have much to learn from each other, but only if the contrasts are raised and the differences between them made explicit. For example, in the last few years, companies in the public services and voluntary sectors have been exposed to market forces, encouraged to compete, to get close to the customer, bust the bureaucracy, dispense with non-core activities and so on. While public services can, indeed need, to learn from the private sector, the differences between them are vital. Simple extrapolation from the world where dilemmas are finally settled by reference to a monetary 'bottom line' damages our schools, our environment, our health and social services.

If private has much to teach public in terms of focus, strategic thinking and change of management, then there is a potential reverse flow in terms of purposes, service, professionalism and accountability. Commercial companies, now desiring to manage via commitment rather than control, might partake from the public service experience of working with professionals to deliver quality services; and also from voluntary organizations, where the energetic contribution of volunteers is often heroic and extraordinary. All big companies can learn about vitality, speed of response and 'natural' learning from small ones, the best of whom have borrowed from their big cousins for years.

We've tried to celebrate the differences between organizations in this book. Learning from one another is not just about best practice, where we seek to clone the apparently successful. Such quick fixes do sometimes work, but, in exploring ways to achieve more learning in the companies that appear in this book—to quote a colleague, David Casey—each of us must reinvent the wheel of our own practice.

Towards the good company?

What is learning for? The question returns time and again. At the outset our ambition extended only to exploring and illustrating learning processes in different sectors of the social economy. Though this was quite enough to be getting on with, it proved impossible to avoid the underlying question. In learning more about how to learn in companies, the responsibility for what is done with that learning also grows.

It is no accident that the interest in learning companies and organizational learning is paralleled by a growing concern with business ethics and issues of right behaviour in public life. One explanation for this is the extent to which old local communities have declined and fragmented (a theme in Chapter 1), while new organizational communities exert increasing power to define what are the right ways to live as well as work:

> Whether we do well, whether we like ourselves, whether we lead happy and productive lives, depends to a large extent on the companies we choose.
>
> Solomon, 1993, p. 148)

This theme is addressed in Chapter 8, and is a preoccupation throughout. Purpose seems particularly important in today's organizations—what is the company for, why does it exist? Many companies are centred on one stakeholder (some, indeed, seem mere extensions of their owners' egos), while others are more mutual and multistakeholder in focus. While shying away from precise definition, the implicit and con-tentious position taken in this book is that the latter are more likely to be 'good companies'.

The notion of a *political economy of learning companies* appeals here because the health and strength of companies and organizations are critical to both the production and the distribution of wealth in a society. Political economy is about the careful management of resources and also about questions of governance—corporate and collective.

The graph below shows company types classified by complexity and purpose. This is an indicative picture, not an authoritative one and not to be taken too literally. It is not possible to say that small company X is simpler in structure or culture than large company Y or that company A serves a higher purpose than company B. But, smaller companies do tend to be simpler and larger ones more complex, and public service companies are among the *most* complex with many conflicting dilemmas, not least the reconciling of national political direction with local voice and accountability as part of ensuring effcient operations. The point is that the political and social impact of companies is as important as the economic, and that these criteria are also important in evaluating organizations and their effects.

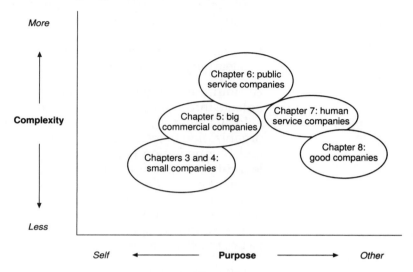

Introduction: A political economy of learning companies

Of course, this is too simple a model with which to pigeonhole individual companies. However, it does seem to have some face validity.

Where would you place your company at present?

What's in this book?

This book addresses 14 main themes, each examined in different contexts, usually in that sector which has gained most experience of this aspect so far. However, we believe all of them to be matters of critical concern for organizations in the 'knowledge era'—sooner or later your company will encounter each of them.

The themes are illustrated with ideas or theories, case histories and applications for you to try out in your own situation. Each contains experiences, approaches and methods for learning. The themes are:

- fragmentation, chaos and learning (Chapter 1)
- what is the learning company? (Chapter 2)
- linking individual and organizational learning (Chapter 3)
- the company as a developing being (Chapter 4)
- future skills (looking forwards) (Chapter 5)
- organizational memory (looking back) (Chapter 5)

- learning from accountability (Chapter 6)
- working with professionals (Chapter 6)
- managing with volunteers (Chapter 7)
- participation in policy making (Chapter 7)
- learning and its consequences (Chapter 8)
- a balanced scorecard (Chapter 8)
- composing the company (Chapter 9)
- a learning society (Chapter 9).

As indicated in the graph earlier, these 14 themes form a linkage through the nine main chapters of this book.

In Chapter 1, The post-modern jigsaw, a social and organizational scene characterized by problems, uncertainty and fragmentation is set. Authorities admit to confusion and learning emerges as a way forward.

Chapter 2, In the age of learning, defines some terms for the rest of the book—what do we mean by learning, organizational learning and the learning company?

The central chapters of the book then address seven key issues in organizational learning, namely:

- the linkage between individual and organizational learning (Chapter 3)
- the phases of the lifecycle, or biography, of the organization and how these affect its development (Chapter 4)
- the organization as a stock of knowledge and skills that must be retained and added to by building organizational memory and acquiring future skills (Chapter 5)
- the problems of creating quality service in the community through the twin themes of accountability and building managerial/professional partnerships (Chapter 6)
- the challenges facing voluntary organizations and their experience in managing with volunteers and with developing participation in policy making (Chapter 7)
- what learning is for and what its consequences are—a balanced scorecard or social audit can help companies to look to the top line—not *just* to the bottom one—and offer great opportunities for new learning (Chapter 8)
- the big picture—composition rather than fragmentation and considering the place of companies in the wider community (Chapter 9).

The learning company idea is only brought to life in a specific context—there is no blueprint. The issues and themes in this book are considered in the context of particular companies—small ones in Chapters 3 and 4, big ones in Chapter 5, public service in Chapter 6, and voluntary organizations in Chapter

7—because all these different organizational types play significant parts in our lives. Contrary to some popular perceptions, economic activity is not confined to the commercial sector; all these types of companies and more besides go to make up the social economy. They have much to learn from each other.

However, you may well be most interested in just *one* type of company—your own. Facilitating organizational learning requires *thought* at the level of the whole and *action* at the locale, where it can make a difference.

Each chapter in this book—apart from the first and the last—contains learning activities to help you consider the implications of these issues, themes and stories and decide what can be done to improve the learning in your company. Taking these activities as the core, the book becomes an organizational self-development manual.

Who is this book for?

People interested in learning companies—understanding them, creating them, working in them—and those who are committed to their own personal self-development. These two impulses go together: such companies need people who are pursuing their own further learning, and only learning organizations are fit to house self-developers.

Despite the complexity of some of the material, this aims to be a reader-friendly book. We hope you will find it accessible and engaging. It contains four types of presentation:

- *text* ideas, arguments and theory; introductions to the type of company featured in the chapter together with the particular challenges and dilemmas that form the learning opportunities in this context
- *stories* cases and illustrations taken from actual companies—some only a few lines in length, others in much more depth
- *pictures* diagrams, figures, cartoons to support the ideas and argument
- *applications* activities and reflective tasks designed to help you apply the ideas to your company and your practice.

We hope you enjoy the book and that it inspires you to action and learning.

References

Hughes, M., (March 1995) 'Propogating the Learning Organization', *Financial Training Review*

Lloyd, T. (1990) *The Nice Company: Why nice companies make more profits*, Bloomsbury, London

Solomon, R. (1993) *Ethics and Excellence: Cooperation and integrity in business*, Oxford University Press, Oxford

1 The post-modern jigsaw

A four-year old was holding his head in his hands and sighing deeply, saying to himself over and over 'Oh dear, Oh no, Oh dear'. Going over to him, the teacher saw that he had covered his sheet of paper with separate irregular shapes. 'Whatever's the matter Michael?' she asked. 'Oh ... !', he said, 'I've drawn this jigsaw but I *just can't do it.*'

We seem to be at the end of something, but if we are the start of something new, we are not sure what it is.

Old certainties, moral values, great institutions are crumbling; there are flashes and glimpses of new possibilities, but they are ephemeral, insubstantial.

Using the telephone, fax, PC we can communicate with a global interest group community, but it's hard to find the time to visit family and friends.

Medical researchers have successfully transplanted heart cells from a baby mouse into an adult mouse. Science can achieve remarkable results, but ...

Parents on a radio news programme talk of how their young son enjoys the *William* books by Richmal Compton and then of the difference between then and now. 'Wherever William went people knew who he was and looked out for him. Now we know our immediate neighbours but no one else. We don't know when he will be old enough for us to let him go out on his own.'

Is it just in our time, now, that our views of the future are so gloomy, so pessimistic? Or is it just that, as Dan Quayle once put it, 'We're on the way to somewhere ... but that may change'.

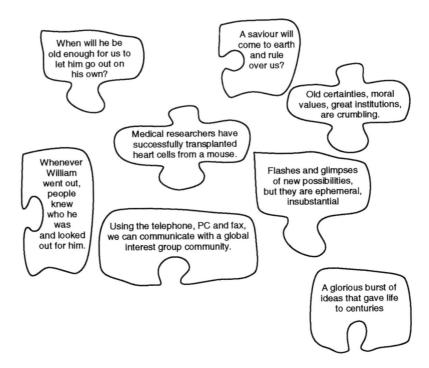

Figure 1.1   The post-modern jigsaw

**Glimmers,
glimpses,
whispers ...**

In a brief life, Massaccio changed the way the Florentines painted. He brought movement, naturalness—part of a glorious burst of ideas that gave life to centuries of humanism. Was there a time when we did not have this drive to progress?

Newspaper polls taken in Britain, the USA, Germany and Japan in 1994 showed the British to be the most gloomy about the future, with 60 per cent believing things would be *worse* in 5 years' time and only 13 per cent believing they would be *better*. The most optimistic country was Japan, but even there, the pessimists are a sizeable majority.

In *The Pursuit of the Millenium*, Norman Cohn observes that chilliastic sects (those which believe that a saviour will come to Earth and rule over us) rise in popularity in times of political or social unrest, and particularly towards the ends of centuries.

Q What do you get if you cross a post-modernist with a member of the Mafia?
A An offer you can't understand.

Bits and pieces, bits and pieces

Life comes in slices—chopped, fragmented. Splintering and splitting seem the order of the day—the United Nations into blocs; continents into nation states; nations into regions, tribes, religions or parties; neighbourhoods into households.

In economic life, some of the vast industrial machine-like organizations are shrinking, splitting, breaking down into parts. In Britain, the national public services are fragmenting into the local management of schools, separate hospital trusts, the dividing of purchaser and provider, even the parcelling off in bits of British Rail.

Douglas Hague forsees the twenty-first-century business environment as being a 'new world disorder', shot through with fragmentation—of markets, with products and brands differentiated by price, quality and prestige; of spending patterns, as individuals seek to 'buy' their own lifestyles; of 'cellular' households with independent individuals who do not even eat together any longer:

> It is not simply that society is becoming increasingly fragmented. The twenty-first century is also likely to see an increase in isolation, if not loneliness, for individuals.
>
> (1994, pp. 12–14)

Even the self is split. Not so much divided as shredded into a host of selves who may or may not form a familial whole. In *The Saturated Self*, Kenneth Gergen describes how the technological achievements of the past century—in radio, transport, telecommunications, computing, etc.—have exposed us to a barrage of social stimulation and produced a radical shift in our exposure to each other:

> Small and enduring communities, with a limited cast of significant others, are being replaced by a vast and ever-expanding array of relationships.
>
> (1991, p. xi)

In this world, there is no such thing as the *true* self:

> The post-modern sensibility questions the concept of a 'true' or 'basic' self, and the concomitant need for personal coherence or consistency. Why, the post-modern asks, must one be bound by any traditional marker of identity—profession, gender, ethnicity, nationality and so on?
>
> (1991, p. 178)

Indeed, to use these old identity tags begins to look restricted and narrow:

> ... the disappearance of 'true self' encourages one to search for the kinds of persons or situations that will enable the various actors in one's ensemble to play their parts. One requires a supporting cast for the Hamlet ... or the emerging Juliet ... For the post-modern, social complicity and identity walk hand in hand; without others there is no self.'
>
> (1991, p. 178)

One—if we can use that term—becomes a pastiche personality engaged in fragmentary relationships. Billy, no longer a Liar, comes of age with Walter Mitty. What can we do with the bits? So often, our attempts to make one thing better sometimes make something else worse.

Welcome to the chaotic world!

Long-held assumptions about the nature of organizing are being questioned. Managing as a constant striving for order and control, of well-structured internal relationships married to a balanced fit of company and environment as part of a planned strategy for a predictable future all, increasingly, belong to a mythical Golden Age. Order resembles death.

Leaving behind the era of 'contingency theories', which sought to specify the variables that stand between actions and outcomes, the relationship between cause and effect now seems so convoluted and complex as to make linear causality virtually untraceable.

But, if adaptation to environmental demands to achieve a stable equilibrium is a song of the dinosaurs, simple randomness leaves us at the mercy of chaos. The paradox has to be held. Hope lies in creativity and innovation short of randomness. Chaos theory is sensationally incompatible with the management textbooks. It suggests that we move

from ...	to ...
policy which is about setting long-term strategic plans and implementing them, moving the company forwards by error detection and correction	... recognizing that, beyond the short term, the effects of our actions are unknowable; 'errors' may be innovations
leadership in the form of will and intent, establishing and realizing new visions and strategic directions	... letting it happen, realizing new direction comes not through prior intent but through a process of learning from what happens

management in terms of order and control of all structures and procedures

... seizing the dynamic, recognizing the multiplicity of choices, orchestrating the debate and managing the political decision processes

culture as shared by everyone, clear, strong 'social glue', instantly recognizable from the outside

... diversity, celebrating differences, containing all sorts of possibilities and inclinations as yet unthought of

success being measured in terms of staying ahead of the game and the competition; the unit of survival is the company

... contributing to a changing world—we create the world as well as being part of it.

And disorder?

Chaos, complexity, paradox and dilemma are just other ways of understanding the order of things. Any way of ordering closes down other possibilities. Some of our confusion arises because we have liberated ourselves from a particular way of knowing based on the rational, 'scientific'. Though disorientating, this is also exciting—a different way of seeing opens up the new, enabling us to do that which we could not do before.

In *The Order of Things*, Foucault quotes, from a short story by Borges, a classification of the animal kingdom from an ancient Chinese encyclopedia (Townley, 1993):

(a) belonging to the Emperor
(b) embalmed
(c) tame
(d) sucking pigs
(e) sirens
(f) fabulous
(g) stray dogs
(h) included in the present classification
(i) innumerable
(j) drawn with a fine camel hair brush
(k) *et cetera*
(l) having just broken the water pitcher
(m) that from a long way off look like flies.

Now what can you do with that?

Problems, yes; solutions, maybe

Recognition of the dangers of child abuse has led to special advice for those working with children and young people. Scout leaders, for example, are advised:

You must never be alone with a young person .... Always try to have someone with you or make sure that others are in earshot or preferably vision. Such actions as touching, talking on a one to one basis, hugging and comforting a distressed youngster is now done at your peril.

(*Scouting*, in *The Guardian*, April 1994)

A young man starts a youth club on a large housing estate. Over 200 13 to 17-year-olds enrol. However, as part of their new financial awareness, schools have begun to charge for the use of their accommodation by community groups. The charge for the youth club is £48.50 per hour, so, for the 3 hours the club runs, the cost is almost £150 a night. The youth club is closed.

'Inefficient' firms downsize, restructure, become flatter, leaner in order to survive, compete and succeed. All these moves result in fewer jobs in the communities where the companies are located. Former staff often can't get other jobs; young school-leavers go straight to unemployment. Government tax revenues cannot keep up with the costs of sustaining these unproductive lives.

The Mtera Dam in central Tanzania is one of the few projects of its kind to be generally judged as a success. It has created a huge power resource and acted as a spur to economic development. However, the population explosion on the shores of the dam, the rapid deforestation for domestic fuel (the villagers are not connected to the electricity) and the lack of infrastructure of roads and communications, were all unforeseen. Wildlife advisers were not involved in the planning and large numbers of crocodiles, monkeys and elephants, attracted to the water, devastate villagers' crops. Officials remain optimistic: 'Let's not eat each other's liver', says one, 'Let's go back and resolve these problems.'

What is right for each part, is wrong for the whole

For years now, Reg. Revans has been warning us about the limitations of experts and the knowledge they deal in. His 'action learning' process focuses on 'problems', not on 'puzzles' (which have 'solutions'):

> Thus the problem is the domain of the leader; unlike the puzzle, it is charged with *unanswerable* questions as well as *unformulated* ones ...

(1982, p. 712)

Argyris, who, along with Revans, has so often put his finger on the heart of the matter, starts his analysis with the following words:

> The message stated herein is full of puzzles, inconsistencies,

dilemmas and paradoxes. The reason for stating this message is that I want to alert the readers to stop taking for granted practices that are accepted as correct that, when examined carefully, are not.

(1990, p. 1)

Over the years, Argyris has collected 'Seven Worldwide Errors', two of which are that:

Actions intended to increase understanding and trust often produce misunderstanding and mistrust.

and that

People do not behave reasonably, even when it is in their best interest.

(1990, pp. 6–8)

Writers on management and organization are currently grappling with the failure of expertise, rationality, solutions and quick fixes. Peters (1992) describes the marketplace as having 'turned ephemeral', requiring us to do the same if we are to deal with 'the fast, fleeting, fickle'. 'If you don't feel crazy, you're not in touch with the times.'

Hampden-Turner sees decision makers as being faced with multiple dilemmas, the horns of which offer the choice of good or good—the differentiation of parts *or* the integration of wholes? Good profits now *or* a long-term orientation? For the private firms, profit is a great reconciler, though there are problems even here:

The limitation of profit as currently conceived is that it strips the profiting person away from his or her environment and allows the first to 'gain' notionally at the expense of the second.

(1990, p. 241)

No such simple reconciler exists outside the market for the many strategic dilemmas to be found in the public services, for example:

Schools cannot decide to stop educating five year olds. The health service cannot refuse to treat patients in Sussex. Yet a private company can easily withdraw from markets, or reduce its product range.

(Haigh, 1993)

Senge makes systems thinking his fifth (and chief) discipline because:

From a very early age we are taught to break apart problems, to fragment the world. This apparently makes complex tasks and subjects more manageable, but we pay an enormous price.

(1990, p. 3)

and:

> We are literally killing ourselves by our inability to think in wholes.

His 'Tragedy of the Commons' is a motif of the times. Two weeks before Christmas 1994, the US National Marine Fisheries Service closed down the famous Georges Bank off the New England coast to fishing. For 20 years, stocks of cod, haddock and flounder have declined, yet the fishermen have resisted limitations. Now the same anguished fishermen complain that the Government should have taken action years ago. In the USA's Western states, ranchers graze cattle on 270 million acres of public land, for which they pay lower fees than on private ranges. This has caused overgrazing and is damaging the land, yet the ranchers put pressure on their senators to block any price rises.

Such stories are increasingly commonplace; they have in common the conflict between individual self-interest and the wider public good. This worsens as fragmentation increases. In the UK, rising numbers of the self-employed lower the take for employer-deducted pay-as-you-earn taxes. For the newly self-employed, a relatively painless way of paying public dues has been replaced by a personal choice—in effect, they decide how much tax to pay (and how much to avoid by taking out pension plans, tax-exempt savings schemes and so on). Individuals, even when they would benefit from better public services or conserved resources, make personal decisions that actually damage these things.

'Why should I make the personal sacrifice while others rip off the state?' The end result is the impoverishment of us all—the tragedy of the commons.

Where are we to turn when all the experts are confused?

Handy has had cause to reflect on the confusion that seems to characterize our times:

> So many things, just now, seem to contain their own contradictions, so many good intentions to have unintended consequences, and so many formulae for success to carry a sting in their tail. Paradox has almost become the cliché of our times.

For example:

> The ideas of *The Age of Unreason* (published four years earlier) are still relevant, therefore; organizations will become both smaller and bigger at the same time; they will be flatter, more flexible and more dispersed; our working lives will, likewise, have to be flatter and more flexible. Life will be unreasonable, in the sense that it won't go on like it used to; we shall have to make things happen for us rather than wait for them to happen. *What I had not anticipated, however, in that first book, was the confusion which this would cause; that the opportunity for personal fulfilment which I so confidently predicted would be complicated by the pressures of efficiency, that the new freedoms would often mean less equality and more misery, and that success might carry a disproportionate price.*
>
> (1994, pp. 2–3; our emphasis)

For those with readily saleable skills, independence from organizations can be liberating. For 'home workers' on pay as low as £1 an hour, it may feel more like imprisonment.

Where shall we look for ways forward? Surprisingly there is something that seems to crop up in much of the recent literature. Revans and Argyris again:

> In any epoch of rapid change those organizations unable to adapt are soon in trouble, and adaptation is only achieved by learning, namely, by being able to do tomorrow, what might have been unnecessary today ... The organization that continues to express only the ideas of the past is not learning, and training systems intended to develop our young may do little more than make them proficient in yesterday's technique.
>
> (Revans, 1983, p. 11)

> We are realizing that in order to achieve organizational excellence, learning, competence and justice are a much more realistic foundation than are morale, satisfaction and loyalty. The first foundation [is] learning.
>
> (Argyris, 1990, p. xi)

Senge sees teaching as one of the main responsibilities of leaders:

'Leader as Teacher' is not about 'teaching' people how to achieve their vision. It is about fostering learning, for everyone ... It is impossible to reduce natural leadership to a set of skills or competencies. Ultimately people follow people who believe in something and have the abilities to achieve results in the service of those beliefs. Or, to put it another way, who are the natural leaders of learning organizations? They are the learners.

(1990, pp. 356–60)

Learning is more implicit in Handy, who offers the three senses of 'continuity', 'connection' and 'direction' as a means of making sense of paradox and the search for meaning. He does not have Senge's faith in leaders and is closer to Revans and Argyris in this respect:

The hope lies in the unknown, in that second curve, if we can find it. The world is up for reinvention in so many ways. Creativity is born of chaos. ... Change comes from small initiatives which work, initiatives which, imitated, become the fashion. We cannot wait for great visions from great people, for they are in short supply at the end of history.

(1994, pp. 270–1)

Not content with learning organizations, Fullan, an educationalist, calls for a 'learning society', one in which we are 'students cum citizens':

We know increasingly more what learning should focus on, and how people learn. The necessary combination of intellectual development ... and social development ... is becoming more evident. The abilities to think and present ideas on the one hand, and to work with others on the other hand are being recognized by education and businesses alike as central to the world's future. Permeating these twin responses is a third purpose—the positive disposition to keep on learning in the face of constant change and societal complexity. Put another way, the ability to cope with change, learning as much as possible with each encounter is the generic capacity needed for the twenty-first century.

(1993, p. 136)

Approaching the millenium, learning is become the conduit for our hopes.

But if learning is an answer, what is this learning *for*? For individuals and companies to improve their skills so that they may lower fish stocks faster? To enhance their capacity to sell sugary, fatty substances to children? To increase profits by reducing employment still further? It's a competitive world—those are the rules of the game.

We won't get out of this one by continuous improvement—by learning to be better at what we already do. We have to change the rules of the game and find new ways of reconciling individual success with public good.

References

Argyris, C. (1990) *Overcoming Organizational Defences: Facilitating organizational learning*, Allyn & Bacon, Boston

Foucault, M. (1970) *The Order of Things*, Tavistock, London

Fullan, M. (1993) *Change Forces: Probing the depths of educational reform*, Falmer Press, Brighton

Gergen, K. (1991) *The Saturated Self*, HarperCollins Publishers, New York

Hague, D. 'The Business Environment of the Twenty-first Century', in Boot, R., Lawrence, J. and Morris, J. (Eds) (1994) *Managing the Unknown: By creating new futures*, McGraw-Hill, Maidenhead

Haigh, D. (1993) *Transforming the Dinosaurs*, Demos, London

Hampden-Turner, C. (1990) *Charting the Corporate Mind*, Blackwell, Oxford

Handy, C. (1994) *The Empty Raincoat*, Hutchinson, London

Peters, T. (1992) *Liberation Management: Necessary disorganization for the nanosecond nineties*, Macmillan, London

Revans, R. W. (1982) *The Origins and Growth of Action Learning*, Chartwell-Bratt, Bromley

Revans, R. W. (1983) *The ABC of Action Learning*, Chartwell-Bratt, Bromley

Scouting, in *The Guardian* (1 April 1994)

Senge, P. (1990) *The Fifth Discipline*, Doubleday Currency, New York

Townley, B. (1993) 'Foucault, Power/Knowledge and its Relevance for Human Resource Management', *Academy of Management Review*, 18 (2), pp. 518–45

2　In the age of learning

The learning company arrives

The learning company is to the 1990s what excellence was to the 1980s. We know now about the problem with excellence—even before the end of that decade, many of Peters and Waterman's 'excellent' companies had ceased to be so.

How can we learn to *stay* excellent? (And how can we learn not to repeat history with any new 'solution'?) Already, by March 1990, Kiechel the mainstream business magazine *Fortune* was saying:

> The old bureaucratic command-and-control model, even in its current decentralised, supposedly lean and mean version, won't be up to the challenges ahead: it won't be fast enough ... keen enough ... (or) smart and sensitive enough.

Bureaucracy-busting is not enough—that's official. The article goes on to question, and then to answer:

> ... is what they (the big companies) actually need a new kind of organization that accommodates radical change, indeed that builds in the capacity to thrive on change? ... In the intellectual gropings of thinkers on these questions—consultants, business school professors, even some reflective managers and executives—the dim outlines of just such a paradigm are beginning to take shape. Call it, for want of a better name, the learning organization.
>
> (Kiechel, 1990)

Well, a better name we think is the learning company, after Pedler, Burgoyne and Boydell (1991, p. 1) who reclaim the old idea of a company as a group of people engaged in a joint enterprise. We use this term to apply to schools or housing departments just as much to engineering or retail 'companies'.

According to Pedler, Burgoyne and Boydell, the learning company is:

> ... an organization that facilitates the learning of all its members *and* continuously transforms itself.
>
> (1991, p. 1)

That 'continously' sounds a bit tiring (if it was *continuously* transforming, would it ever *be* anything?), but we get the idea; the learning company implies the:

- continuous learning and the development of potential in all the people who work with the company (and also of the people who work for the company's main trading partners and allies)
- self-development of the company as a whole organization, including the integration of each individual's learning with that of the company as a whole.

This is a tall order, but many are working on it now—all over the world. Given the resources and the will, the first of these is not so difficult—the technologies and methods for encouraging all staff in continuous learning and development exist—but the second remains much more mysterious and challenging. Most companies working with the idea of the learning company are interpreting it mainly in the light of individual learning opportunities. Although this is sensible—given the difficulties, conceptual and otherwise, of the second—no amount of *individual* development will alone produce an organization able to change itself as a whole. The learning company is *not* the training company:

> ... it is clear that organizational learning is not the same thing as individual learning, even when the individuals who learn are members of the organization. There are too many cases in which organizations know *less* than their members. There are even cases in which the organization cannot seem to learn what every member knows.
>
> (Argyris and Schon, 1978, p. 9)

Or, to put it more simply:

> How can a team of committed managers with individual IQs above 120 have a collective IQ of 63?
>
> (Senge, 1990, p. 9)

When was the last time you were in this situation? Last year? Last month? Last week?

What do we mean by 'learning' anyway?

It's fantastic! Being on this project has allowed me to learn lots of skills.

It always takes me time to get used to new ideas but I'm always ready to try.

I found it hard to learn at first, very frustrating, it seemed as if what I knew wasn't worth anything any more.

Application 1: My individual learning at work

1. Think back to a time recently when you learned something useful about yourself or the work you do or the people you work with. Describe, in a few words:

- *What did I learn?*

_____

_____

_____

- *How did I learn it?*

_____

_____

_____

- *Which factors helped me to learn*

_____

_____

_____

- *What changed as a result? How do I know that I have learned?*

_____

_____

_____

2. Now think of a time when you resisted learning, for example:

- by not accepting suggestions from a colleague
- because learning is not encouraged or rewarded where you work
- ignoring feedback from someone
- persisting in doing something *your* way when others have adopted different methods
- because you don't have the time and so on. Ask yourself:

- *What did I resist learning?*

_____

_____

_____

- *Why did I resist it?*

_____

_____

_____

- *Which factors hindered my learning?*

_____

_____

_____

3. Finally, summarize the factors that help or hinder your learning—include those *within* yourself as well as those from outside.

Factors that help or hinder my learning

	Help	Hinder
In me		
Outside me		

Source: Aspinwall, *et al.*, 1992

> As I've got older, I've learned that it's difficult to give good advice to people. You have to ask a lot of questions.

> I'm working in this excellent team. We really spark off each other.

If we are in the 'age of learning', then we had better get our language straight. What do we *mean* by 'learning' or when we say someone 'has learned'? Look at the quotes above. Learning can involve skills, new ideas, frustration, difficulty and getting older. There are often strong feelings involved here—feeling fantastic, not knowing anything worth while, hardship, frustration again, excellence, excitement and enjoyment.

With the arrival of the learning company, learning—in people and in the company as a whole—becomes a major concern for managers and leaders. The linking of individual with organizational learning is a particular concern. Let's look first at what we mean by individual learning. Start by thinking about a time recently when you feel that you learned something about yourself or your work (see Application 1).

Learning is such an integral part of life that it is often inseparable. George Kelly, whose Personal Construct Psychology holds that we cannot know the world directly, but that we experiment with it on a continuous basis, understanding it via our unique 'personal constructs' said:

> Man lives best when he commits himself to getting on with his life. Since I see the concept of learning as nothing less than this, the term seems redundant when applied to a living creature.
>
> (1969, p. 65)

Kelly was writing in the 1950s, but some of his ideas are very relevant today. In his emphasis on commitment to action and the notion of living as learning, he shares much with founders of the learning organization idea such as Reg. Revans. However, for our purposes, we *do* need to separate learning from living. When such a premium is placed on learning, we need to make a special study of it, not least to help people who find it hard. This includes all of us at times, and there are many people in our society—children and adults—with 'learning difficulties'. Now that living requires so much learning, these learning difficulties become even more tragic, denying people the chance of work, the opportunity to live independent lives and, perhaps above all, to become fully human.

What we mean by learning has changed over time. The definition of learning taught in the 1960s:

> learning is a, more or less permanent, change in behaviour as a result of experience

seemed a bit unsatisfactory then. Had we known about Kelly, not to mention Dewey, Jung, Rogers and others, we would have known how much our teachers had, at that time, been captured by the behaviourists.

Although there is no universally agreed definition of learning today, one simple way of putting it is that learning is about *how we change*. After learning, we are different in some way from the way we were before. In the learning company, four kinds or types of learning are important—we can learn:

1 *about* things (or *knowledge*)
2 to *do* things (or *skills, abilities, competencies*)
3 to *become ourselves, to achieve our full potential* (or *personal development*)
4 to *achieve things together* (or *collaborative enquiry*)

The four types of learning

The first two of these types—knowledge and skills, abilities, competencies—are familiar and have been recognized as important in the best companies for many years. The third type—personal development—has been valued *outside* the world of work, in schools and in adult education, but is now becoming increasingly important in organizations. The fourth type—collaborative enquiry—is less familar, yet it is one of the keys to organizational learning, something we are only just beginning to recognize.

Of course, this is not the only way of defining learning, but it is useful to recognize that people are often talking about different things when they use the word. The classification used here seems to cover the main meanings in use:

• *Knowledge* Learning *about* things covers a wide spectrum of knowledge and understanding, from the memorizing of simple facts to the deep understanding of complicated ideas. This ranges from knowing 'this' or 'that' to knowing 'why', which is a very different matter, and, for many purposes, we should need to break this category down further.
• *Skills, abilities, competencies* are about learning to *do* things. This category includes our mental and manual skills, our abilities with other people and our competence in certain situations.

These first two types of learning will be familiar, used in

such pairings as knowledge and skills, theory and practice, and implied in the distinction, academic and vocational. The behaviourist view of learning has useful things to say about these types of learning, about the importance of clear objectives, sequence, demonstration, practice and feedback.

Surprisingly often, these two types of learning are unconnected and split off from each other. For example, some people still believe that we can identify whether or not young people are 'academic' or 'vocational' and can use this diagnosis to plan the rest of their formal education. In the organizational world, Henry Mintzberg, among others, has been very critical of business schools, especially where inexperienced would-be managers are taught a lot of 'know-that' on MBA programmes. Reg. Revans has long railed against the split between knowing and doing and his action learning aims to bind the two inextricably:

> There is no learning without action, and no (sober and deliberate) action without learning.

Instead of the Master of Business Administration conferred on those who acquire a lot of 'know-that' without the experience and 'know-how', Revans has suggested—not entirely mischievously—that MBA stands for 'Moral Bankruptcy Assured'. Doing and action confer a moral responsibility on us that, perhaps, the possession of knowledge alone does not—a view echoed in Iris Murdoch's 'learning is moral progress' (1992).

The separation becomes more of a nonsense in the context of our third type of learning.

- *Personal development* involves nothing less than the aim to *become ourselves, to achieve our full potential.* Here we have notions of 'ages and stages'—levels of development linked with various ages. Learning *within* stages is more *incremental*, whereas moving *between* stages—from crawling to walking; from being a professional to becoming a manager; from being a 'controller' to becoming a 'facilitator'—requires more of a step-jump or *transformation*.

With the notion of lifelong learning, the ideas of biography and 'andragogy' (Malcolm Knowles' word for adult learning) can be added to the lessons of pedagogy. Andragogy concerns itself not only with intellectual and competency development, but also with questions of purpose and identity.

As yet, none of the main schools of learning theory have much to say about our last type—learning to *achieve things together*. Learning is generally seen as something individuals do on their own, happening, somehow, inside them. Suppose that learning can also take place *between* people, in the spaces or relationships between individuals.

- *Collaborative enquiry* is about learning to *achieve things together*, cooperating in collective learning. Action learning and similar recent developments in adult and management learning aim at this, where outcomes cannot be fully measured in terms of what individuals take away, *but by what is created together*.

Surprisingly enough, although this last type of learning seems very new, various historical precedents can be found. Samuel Hartlib (1600–1662) and his associates proposed an early sort of learning community with the 'Office of Addresses' for the spreading of scientific knowledge during the ferment of the Commonwealth Parliament. He and his associates often published anonymously or collaboratively under one name because their work was 'all in a knot of one another's labours'.

Collaborative enquiry forms the bridge from individual learning to the learning company. Understanding it better will help us to transform ourselves as a whole organization. We know already that some companies create better conditions for this sort of learning than others—they have a better 'learning climate', they encourage people to take time out to learn, they value learning as being at the heart of the enterprise.

This brief sketch shows how definitions of learning change over time. What we understand now is different from what was understood in 1950, especially with regard to the second two types of learning. What will learning mean to us in 10 or 20 years' time?

Organizational learning

... learning has become the key developable and tradable commodity of an organization

(Garratt , 1987, p. 10)

Learning disabilities are tragic in children ... They are no less tragic in organizations, where they also go largely undetected.

(Senge, 1990, p. 18)

In considering organizational learning and what is meant by that, first think about how your organization encourages and welcomes learning (or not).

Application 2: My learning in my company

1. What—of significance—have you learned at work over the last 12 months?

_____

_____

_____

2. Who else in the organization knows that you have learned this?

_____

_____

_____

3. Has the company learned from your learning?

Yes, a great deal ☐

Yes, a little ☐

No ☐

Don't know ☐

Organizational learning is a relatively new concept, but, again, not that new. There is a voluminous literature reaching back at least to the late 1960s that has rapidly expanded since the late 1980s. The terms 'learning organization' and 'learning company' stem from the notion of a 'learning system' discussed by Revans in 1969 (Revans, 1982) and Schon in 1970 (Schon, 1971). There are earlier precursors—notably Gregory Bateson.

How can an organization be said to learn? This is as difficult as the previous question of how people learn. For a start, it calls into question what we mean by 'organization'. One of the great contributions to the literature is Argyris and Schon's 'What is an organization that it may learn?' (1978, Chapter 1).

It helps when we use _organic_ rather than _machine_ metaphors to think about organizations. Organizational learning and notions such as the learning company become easier to grapple with if we think of organizations as living organisms. Machines are inanimate and programmed; organisms are alive and can learn.

The link between individual and organizational learning is now a pressing concern. Companies need to learn in order to survive and flourish, and, beyond the needs of particular entities, the many human problems of environment, poverty, inequality and lawlessness can only be resolved through worldwide collaboration and organization.

How can the company learn from everyone? And how can organizations learn about organizing? How we can attach the two strands of individual and organizational learning to create better wholes (see Figure 2.1).

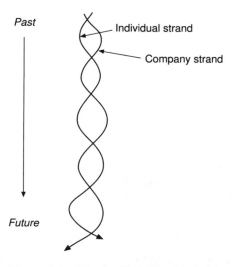

Figure 2.1   The double helix of individual and organizational learning

We give some examples of where this has been done successfully in later chapters, but how can we organize in such a way that it comes naturally?

One thing that emerges from the discussion so far is that it helps if we begin to understand learning as being, at least in part, *a property of relationship*. Human resources managers and other 'people specialists' in organizations have usually focused on individuals—recruiting, selecting, training, appraising, career planning and even retiring and sacking them. Although it includes all the forms of *individual* learning, the learning company is, ultimately, about learning *relationships*. As noted above, this means that we must study what goes on *between* people and not just think of learning as a property of the individual person alone. Like the fabled psychologist, we have been searching under that particular lamp-post because that was where the light was, where we knew most:

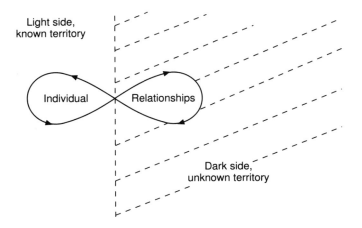

Figure 2.2   Learning in organizations—light and dark sides

What are the possibilities for learning in groups, networks, organizations? What is learning in company? These are central questions to which we keep returning in this book.

Two types of organizational learning

As noted earlier, learning can be experienced as incremental or as transforming. This distinction is also useful in thinking about what we mean by organizational learning. Are we

- improving, or ...
- transforming?

Improving is incremental or single-loop learning—the continuous improvement of the Total Quality movement. In the developmental stage model of the small learning company (see Chapter 4), this is learning done *within* stages. The key question here is, how can we do this better?

Transforming is 'step-jump' or double-loop learning, that is, radically changing what we do, a caterpillar-to-butterfly-type of movement. In the stage model of the small learning company, this is the learning required *between* stages. The key questions here are, should we do this at all and what shall we do that is completely different?

Time for a story.

> **The Ship of Theseus**
> During a voyage, Theseus gradually renewed and refurbished his ship by removing a plank at a time and replacing it with new timber. The old planks were thrown overboard. As the planks were removed piecemeal and each part replaced by one that was the same only newer, those on board had no sense of the ship changing in any fundamental way. Did Theseus thus create a new ship or recreate the same ship with new materials?
>
> The story is further complicated by the fact that, as Theseus sailed, another group of people followed behind and collected the planks that were thrown overboard. They used the discarded parts to reconstruct an exact replica of the original ship using the original parts. The two ships sailed into harbour one after the other. Which was the original? Which ship can be called the 'same ship'?

Is this incremental or transformational learning? Er, pass. However, the story does show that organizations—unlike individual humans—can change bit by bit over time until they are, in a way, entirely new. From day one, each new person learns, intentionally and unintentionally, from co-workers about their organization. What the new person learns is dependent on the preceding generation, but they also bring their learning from outside the organization, that is, something new.

Another thing that seems clear is that if Theseus had attempted a step-jump, caterpillar-to-butterfly transformation out there on the Aegean, his story would probably never have been written. How can organizations 'under full sail' attempt to transform themselves quickly?

Finally, organizational learning—as with individual learning—involves changes of identity. Gradually or suddenly, we become different, but not, perhaps, entirely so.

A company of learners?

So far, we've discussed individual and organizational learning. What of societal learning? Sometimes it is easier to understand organisms from the standpoint of their environment. We can enhance our understanding of individuals as learners by looking at them in the context of the learning company. We will perhaps understand this idea better by considering it within the context of a learning society—an issue we touch upon in the final chapter.

In terms of organizational learning and how to manage it, a first step is to place learning at the centre of the company's value system. In the story that follows, who would you choose to join your company? Our collective, company values often show up most clearly when we are looking for new recruits, people to join us.

Johnson Consulting Engineers

The company was looking for a new principal consultant to join its current team of six. From a 30-year tradition of working in mining, JCE is increasingly diversifying into water and general civil engineering. The founder and Managing Director, Frank Johnson, is interviewing for a final decision between two candidates together with Marsha Page, a Human Resources Consultant.

The first candidate, Darren McKenzie, is tall and well turned out, with a ready smile and a firm handshake. His CV and list of achievements shows early responsibility on a lot of projects, many of them overseas. Marsha notices how he talks about these projects—clearly, confidently and always showing himself to good advantage. Frank catches himself wondering whether JCE can provide the right sort of challenge for someone of Darren's calibre, but he can imagine working well with the young man in taking the firm forwards.

Darren McKenzie is happy with his current firm, but, as one of the biggest in the business and with a reputation for training its people well, there is a lot of competition for promotion and choice of projects. JCE could provide him with more scope to influence the development of the business.

Towards the end of the interview, Marsha asks him:

'What's the most difficult situation you've ever had to handle?'

Darren replies:

'Well, I always look for the positives. There are always those jobs where, however well you are prepared and however well you build exclusions into the contracts, the geology turns out wrong or key people let you down. You can't legislate for those.'

'Yes,' presses Marsha, 'but have you had any failures?' He stiffens just a little, but maintains his steady smile.

'Well, there are a few project opportunities I didn't manage to get, when they might have led to even faster promotion, but I think you'll find that my track record speaks for itself.'

Frank and Marsha spend much longer than they intended with Darren McKenzie, with the result that they are 40 minutes late in welcoming their second candidate. Philip Leslie is a more reserved person who takes time to warm up. In his early forties, he is slim, bespectacled, thinning on top and shows a quick and active mind. He is also with a much larger company than JCE and has an equally impressive CV.

Frank notices that when he talks about the projects he has been involved in, Philip Leslie often mentions the names of the people he worked with and the various qualities they brought to the job. He is aware of his own abilities, but tends to mention them in the context of the job. He asks Frank a lot of questions about the other people at JCE and suggests that it would be useful to meet them all before making any decisions.

When Marsha asks her question about difficulties and failures, she gets a different sort of response. Philip Leslie becomes more animated:

> 'The projects I remember best are those when we were able to sit down as a team and tease out what went wrong and how to put it right. Mistakes are part of this business—they're inevitable—what counts is whether you can learn from them fast enough in order to get the job done ahead of budget and time constraints.'
>
> Marsha persists:
>
> 'But what about *your* mistakes, your personal ones?'
>
> Philip laughs:
>
> 'Yes, indeed, where do you want to start? Usually they're to do with reading people wrong—trusting the one who lets you down—or when I simply get it wrong, perhaps because I'm feeling insecure and decide to play it by the book. However, I reckon never to make the same mistake twice, and sometimes I succeed!'
>
> Frank finds Philip appealing, but worries about his priorities—he seems almost more interested in failures than in successes. He can't picture Philip being a leader in JCE in the same way as he can Darren.
>
> (Based on an idea from Ellen Godfrey's *Murder Behind Closed Doors*, Virago, 1989.)

Choosing a new person to join the company—particularly in a key post—is difficult. Much hangs on making the right decision. We're so happy to delegate some of the responsibility to 'headhunters' when we can. So, who did you pick? The 'winner' or the 'learner'? Can you be an 'excellent' company *and* a 'learning company'?

The learning company idea puts learning and the ability to learn at the heart of its values. In such a company, people are seen as developing beings in their own right and, as our colleague John Burgoyne has pointed out, as learners on behalf of the organization.

References

Argyris, C. and Schon, D. (1978) *Organizational Learning: A theory of action perspective*, Addison-Wesley, Reading, Massachusetts

Aspinwall, K. *et al.* (1992) *Managing Evaluation in Education*, Routledge, London

Garratt, R. (1987) *The Learning Organization*, Fontana, London

Kelly, G. A., 'The Autobiography of a Theory', in Maher, B. (Ed.) (1969) *Clinical Psychology and Personality*, Wiley, New York

Kiechel, W. (1990) 'The Organization That Learns', *Fortune*, 12 March

Murdoch, I. (1992) *Metaphysics as a Guide to Morals*, Chatto & Windus, London

Pedler, M. J., Burgoyne, J. G. and Boydell, T. H. (1991) *The Learning Company: A strategy for sustainable development*, McGraw-Hill, Maidenhead

Revans, R. W. (1982) 'The Enterprise as a Learning System', in Revans, R. W. *The Origins and Growth of Action Learning*, Chartwell-Bratt, Bromley

Schon, D. A. (1971) *Beyond the Stable State*, Random House, New York

Senge, P. (1990) *The Fifth Discipline*, Doubleday Currency, New York

3   Self and company

The tasks of creating a learning climate, fostering learning relationships and linking individual and organizational learning are easier to talk about than to practice. The fragmentation and unconnectedness we sometimes experience in our organizations is one aspect of our post-modern jigsaw and a lack of what has been called 'joined-up thinking'. Like the small child struggling to link the letters the individual crafting of which has been hard-won, we can't get our act together.

Yet, most people who learn something significant and relevant to their work would like to pass this learning on. In our experience, the willingness is usually there, but the confidence to persuade others may not. We think, 'If only my boss had attended this course ... had had this experience ... understood this idea'. At a seminar given by Roger Harrison, a man from the motor trade said, 'If I go back and tell my boss we've been talking about love in organizations, he'll be horrified!' We can well imagine. And that goes for many innovative ideas—whether they are simply daft or just daft and brilliant. The problem lies with how we organize ourselves. If we want to link individual and company learning, then we need to organize in a way that encourages the appropriate actions.

In this chapter, we look at how one individual in one company is addressing this problem.

CASE: Linking individual and organizational learning at Fretwell Downing

Richard is the Managing Director of Fretwell-Downing—a specialist software company employing about 100 people. He began working in the company ten years ago, joining it from the founding organization, which is a catering company. He became MD in 1989, at a time when there was increasing pressure on the company to make considerable changes. He decided that, having learned all he could within the company, he must look outside and, on reflection, decided to take part in an executive MBA.

This story is in three episodes. After each part we 'pause' for reflection and make a few points. Episode 1 is presented in two columns, what Richard does and what happens in the company.

Episode 1: Time out

Richard

I have grown up through various career changes the most major of which was when I switched from the Catering Company to the Computing Company in 1983, literally living by my wits and learning on the backs of everyone else in the company—terrific. And then in 1989 I took over as MD.

I got to the point where I couldn't not learn from anyone around me—but I couldn't learn anything else fundamental. It was going to be incremental learning and it was necessary to break out and it was actually through Mike (a university tutor, we had dinner together and talked about the Executive MBA) . . . I got intrigued.

I suggested that I should go and do the MBA. There was some surprise but there wasn't any resistance to it in the end.

What it gave me most was space outside the company. To be honest when I started in 1990 I had a very, very tough first year.

Fretwell Downing

At that time, the company needed to change. It had grown very rapidly on the back of one particular market sector for education systems. The whole company was skewed around that.

Until then, the culture of the company was that you either learned on the job or brought in new people. On the computer side, we had brought in some very bright Cambridge graduates—it's still part of the folklore, the 'Cambridge syndrome'—and it's still they who are the heart of the company. It was very much a technology-led company. Management training was not on the agenda at all and even technical training was something done almost under duress. We were in a position in those first six to eight years of meteoric growth where we could do that.

. . . in terms of the fact that the company had just grown like Topsy. We'd been through the classic phase of thinking that all the top technical people had to be good as managers and promoted them all to positions of total incompetence in management. Frankly, we hadn't got anybody else anyway, except us caterers who were actually quite good. Caterers tend to be naturally very good managers because they have to make things work to absolute deadlines. Computing doesn't really understand deadlines the way a caterer does. You don't think about it, it's just there.

Because of the Cambridge syndrome and because it was much more marketing than technically led, there was a real battle, mainly between myself and Anthony who was the technical founder of the company. He was not out of a catering background, having a chemistry degree and a doctorate in gas spectroscopy—very much a science background.

So what the MBA gave me ... it was like a holiday, so amazing to stop for 3 days and focus on one thing. I happened to hit an extremely good cohort, 11 or 12 of us. So what it did for me, was reassurance and self confidence. Nobody would ever say that I wasn't a reasonably confident person but it was at a time when it was important to get that confidence because I was trying to give day-to-day leadership to the company.

It was a hodge podge of a company. It didn't understand whether it was a technical company or a product company. My instinct was to simplify and I took it way down the route of strategic business units. I'd got to the point of saying we should split the company up. We were only small anyway, but it seemed to me that we had three separate companies—catering, education systems and libraries—not even supported by central IT people. I said disband them. Of course, at that time was brilliant. It was Tom Peters—*In Search of Excellence*—off we go *now*! Fortunately, it didn't go quite that far. We ran into a cash-flow problem and brought in a financial director, who, to me, was almost as important as the MBA, as he was another non-family director. He gave some balance and had a lot of experience, so it was excellent.

It was reassurance and confidence and being able to check oneself against not only the theory but also in rubbing shoulders with other people in similar positions. There were at least another couple of directors, technical reps and other people from marketing. That was great. I'm a fairly competitive person and it was quite nice to sort of test oneself. To be given marks ... I like it and it's a long time since that has happened.

Here I can get some success, if I personally close a deal. But that isn't the same—the appraisal system works for the staff but we tend not to do it so much for ourselves. I'm quite seriously interested in introducing both peer and upward appraisal perhaps on a confidential basis. I think that would be very positive.

Every assignment was focused back on the company . . . monthly assignments . . . it was fully in your mind at the time. I found most of it very stimulating and I would bring it back.

It was two years and every month there was something, however small or big, a constant feeding back to people on the Board or further down. Part of the stalemate in the company was to do with Anthony's position. He and his brother own the company. The family tradition goes back even before I was around. In some ways I'm more family than not, but I'm not.

A lot of the final sorting out of the company was to do with the transition from Anthony to me. The extra dimension was the confidence— whatever you want to call it—that I was getting from the MBA. There was never any resistance from Anthony, but it was a frame of mind thing. It swung the balance in the company between Anthony and myself on to a level playing field in terms of being marketing *and* technology led rather than marketing alone, which was the route I was taking it down with the SBUs. This route, in the end, would have dissipated the technical excellence, would have fragmented it. We started to get the balance right.

Stop here for a moment and take some time out from the text. Do you recognize any of this so far?

Application 3: What's this got to do with me?

1. Are any aspects of this story familiar to you? Which?

_____

_____

_____

2. Do you recognize any aspects of *yourself* in the story?

_____

_____

_____

3. Do you recognize any aspects of *your organization* in the story? Which are these?

_____

_____

_____

4. What examples can you give of similar things happening in your company or organization?

_____

_____

_____

5. Or, at this point, are you thinking:

'I should be so lucky.'

'My company would never give me the time or resources to do an MBA—or any other kind of training or development for that matter.'

'Nobody would listen. I'm not important enough to feed my learning back into the organization in any meaningful way.'

'The last thing we want around here is any more good ideas!'

'Who *is* Tom Peters?'

or what?

Perhaps you noticed how Richard's learning and that of the company (and that means other people, especially Anthony in this case) are closely coupled. In writing the story, it's sometimes hard to decide where to make the column break. People learn with and from each other, and what comes about in company is a jumble of each other's ideas, emotions and motivations. While we may say that 'so-and-so learned X', this is perhaps more to do with convenience or our tendency for singling out heroes than an accurate reflection of how learning happens.

Secondly, there is the 'coincidence' of Richard's MBA with the company's need to change. The personal learning experience comes opportunely for a company searching for a new direction, struggling to balance an old technological excellence with a new marketing perspective.

Of key importance here is the going out for learning. Richard goes out, recognizing that he could no longer learn anything 'fundamental' on the inside. He takes this time out in another 'company', of learners—a temporary 'organization' of people from different businesses and backgrounds. Here, besides novelty, there is more variety of ideas and experience. However, although he spends this time away, he is always bringing the learning back; his new ideas are linked closely with the work inside.

This going out and returning, looking out and looking in, is one of the basic patterns in learning for both people and organizations. The 'compare and contrast' of the examination question-setter is based on this very old principle, which has something in common with the Hegelian dialectic mentioned in Chapter 2.

If we give a twist to the familiar learning cycle of experience, reflection, making meaning and taking action, we can see it as an inner/outer flow. That is, going *outside* into the world to take action and gain the experience, bringing this back *inside* to reflect and make meaning, going *outside* to test this in action, and so on.

Figure 3.1   The ins and outs of learning

In Richard's story, sometimes it is the company serving as the inner, with the MBA as the outer; at other times Richard is the inner, the company the outer; and, again, at times, Richard forms the inner and Anthony is the outer. What matters is the contrast, even contest, in the relationship and the dialogue between the two.

We could also note here, in the light of earlier remarks about the difficulties companies may find in learning beyond the pioneer stage, the struggle involved in learning, in moving on. Richard himself feels he must move—out to the MBA. Fretwell Downing also has to move beyond what it knows— its mastery of the one market, its scientific and technical expertise—and, yet, much of it wants to stay the same. Donald Schon (1971) has called this 'dynamic conservatism', where we 'fight like mad to stay the same'. This is a sharp example of old competencies becoming the enemy of new learning. It is this dynamic conservatism in people and companies that stops us from learning when we need to move on.

Back to the story.

Episode 2: Back at work

Having gone out of the company to create the conditions for learning, Richard becomes engaged with action in the company. Now, it is not possible to separate his learning and that of others in the company; they are all part of one another.

How does this further diffusion of learning throughout the company happen?

1. *Richard increasingly integrates what he learned from his time out into the company:*

> One of the tools that I came out and used was the early steps of soft systems analysis. As part of taking over from Anthony, I also took on being the general manager on the biggest of the business units. I did a soft systems analysis up to the point of drawing a rich picture. I interviewed all the staff there, I told them what I was trying to do. Then I used that and it was extremely good, for them as well as me. It was played back to them, their views and perceptions of each other. I plagiarized it but I think that's what it's all about.

2. *Other people bring in new questions and ideas:*

> Going back 8 years there wasn't a training budget. It may have been hidden in the personnel budget. It came in with J coming in from the Health Service from a committed accounting approach. He wanted to know how much there was to spend. It was very much a matter of committing a dollop of cash—no questions asked. Very little if any pre-planning. A bit on the technology side. We introduced something called the Learning Company Programme about 18 months ago. Before I was conscious of the books! That was to demonstrate some sort of faith. There was a general sort of upsurge at a time of great change. The idea was much more company-organized learning as opposed to personal learning.

Also:

> I have to say there were acts of faith going on before mine. Julie the Training and Quality Manager and Liz who was my PA had a very valuable view of the company. It may be a female view or a middle manager view which was much more people-oriented than the Board's. They chipped away for a long time and now we've got this nice balance. The original balance was between technology and marketing and now we've got the people balance better. We have always talked about valuing people but what we did was alienate them.

3. *The learning opportunities start to spread:*

> Part of the pressure on a small company is how do you cope with all these young people who want to develop. And that's another terribly important thing we've discovered about the learning company business. There's a common fear that if you invest in people they're going to leave or they're going to want more money, but that has absolutely categorically not been the case here. People have wanted to learn. Some have wanted it to get on with their career and I have to say that MBAs would usually be done because we can see a career progression, but there are an awful lot of other types of learning, not higher or lower, where people are doing it for self-motivation.

4. The boundary between the company itself and the wider world becomes more porous:

> What we've achieved in the last 3 years is amazing in terms of the network. We're a company that is the same size in the number of people, but we're on an order of I don't know what magnitude of influence because of the network of people that we've got. It's less the sales network than the collaborative network in terms of information. We have the ORACLE partnerships in terms of selling the things so, instead of a tiny restricted market, sandwiched between the technology and our people, we've got a global market courtesy of ORACLE who are taking our products to the world. So, we've gone from being this incredibly constrained company to being a 'virtual company'—another lovely expression—but we are a virtual company because we have incredible links through ORACLE to the world and through our technology partners. This is what I'm now calling the learning company, the network or the virtual or the learning company, because where does the company stop?

At the end of Episode 2, Richard has brought his learning back into the company and discovered the learning of lots of other people. At the same time, the company is undergoing great change. Before going on, take a few more minutes for reflection.

Application 4: Conclusions from the story so far

1. Jot down any preliminary conclusions or thoughts that you've had so far. What ideas can you take away with you?

_____

_____

_____

2. Have you written down anything like:

'Everyone should do an MBA.'

'Everyone should read books.'

'Everyone needs time out.'

'All companies need conflict.'

or something else?

_____

_____

_____

Case studies are often designed to teach particular lessons. There used to be a saying in the USA that 'you can't teach a Harvard man anything', meaning, actually, that the archetypal Harvard man (occasionally woman) cannot learn anything new, because—as a result of being taught on the MBA via 1000 case studies in two years—there's nothing left to know.

This is one reason for our calling our cases 'stories'. Stories may carry fairly obvious messages—maybe Red Riding Hood should have been accompanied by a parent—but they are less about teaching lessons, more about stimulating the imagination and encouraging people to make their own meanings. The story of Richard and Fretwell Downing thus provides the material for many possible meanings. Ask yourself about the implications of your conclusions. For example:

- '*Everyone should do an MBA.*' Doing an MBA will stretch most people and create space for the lucky student to have lots of good thoughts and ideas. However, Richard was 'lucky' in several other ways. For a start, as MD, it must be easier for him to put it into practice than someone lower down in the company. Even so, there was a bit of resistance and this may have made him even more determined to apply it and to show its relevance.

    Also, and crucially, the company needed to change, to get new ideas from outside. In a different situation, the manager with her new MBA could become seriously disillusioned if there was no welcome for the new ideas. Another danger is that doing an MBA is likely to be possible for only a few in the company. This can lead to élitism or neglect of other people's learning. And, one last horror scenario, supposing Richard was surrounded by other MBA graduates, all of whom spoke the magic argot of 'corporate strategy' and 'niche marketing'? It's just possible that, in such company, the rush to 'SBU's' *would* have been irresistible!

- '*Everyone should read books.*' Well, yes, we'd certainly agree with that, but many of the above points apply. It depends, too, on your learning style and that of your organization. There are lots of places where you can get ideas. If reading books *guaranteed* learning, it would all be much simpler, but it doesn't and it isn't.

- '*Everyone needs time out.*' Time out is very useful in learning—it allows us to experience something other than our everyday working lives. It can create the outer for the inner to allow dialogue and learning. But, again, time out alone won't do it for you—you need to consciously go out and consciously bring it all back home. In some organizations, 'time outs' have achieved fashion accessory status; no one really expects anything to happen back at work—the edge is gone.

- *'All companies need conflict.'* This is an interesting one. 'Yes,' says Richard Pascale (1990) 'an organization's ability to cope with competition and turbulence outside is a direct consequence of the ability to generate, manage and learn from an appropriate level of conflict on the inside.' Inner and outer again.

  In a sense, all learning arises from something known being challenged by something that might be better, but this is especially so when what is needed is something transformational rather than incremental. If a company is to change its habitual ways of acting, for the better, it's hard to see how this can come about without conflict. Indeed, it probably will not come about unless someone finds the courage to challenge or disagree in the first place. All managers try to create order, and many of us are conflict-averse, preferring to smooth things over. It's natural.

  In this episode, Fretwell Downing found a challenge to the Board's 'business' orientation (itself a recently-won balance between the previously competing technological and marketing forces) and a 'people' perspective. How fortunate for Fretwell Downing that Julie and Liz were willing to make their views known. Or was it?

- 'Etc.' The 'etc.' just demonstrates that there are many other conclusions and meanings you could make. Irritatingly, perhaps, 'it all depends'. We see clear limits to that popular idea of benchmarking best practice when it comes to thinking about learning. It's fine to import those things that *can* be imported—new procedures, methods and practices—but learning involves the whole unique person or organization. In some ways, at least, it has to be invented here. Whatever you take away will be reinvented by you, in your company.

Episode 3: Transformations

Both Richard and the company have undergone changes fundamental enough to be termed transformations. Here the change has not been gradual, incremental, but discontinuous, different. Crucial to these transformations are issues of *relationship*—the relationship of Richard and Anthony, his Chairman and the co-owner of the company, and also the relationship between the company and its trading partners. Interesting, too, is the word 'experiment' and the difficulty Richard has in using this in the context of running a business.

I'm not running this as an experiment. I'm running it because I believe it makes sense. Until such time as I or the company changes its mind, it will carry on. It is so reinforced by what A is now doing in the Management School (Anthony is now Chairman of the University Management School). This is an interesting one. He came out of education in the first place, and came into the company because his father was ill. He then ran the company and has now got back into education, which he enjoys.

But I felt he was the block to me personally doing any training. It was just this culture, which must have come from him, that you didn't need other training, you got it internally. But now it's turned. He uses me and the example of the other MBAs. It's terrific. I suspect it was a culture he picked up from his father. You might find it interesting to get Anthony's view. He now publicly uses my transformation and the others, but we were so bloody close. It was more a father and son relationship, but we are more on a level now.

He's had to go out ... the release on the company ... we didn't have to have complete succession. In other companies he would have gone and that would have been it and you would have lost valuable things. But what we've been able to do is not strategy, but you just had to do it instinctively. He's gone out and got refreshed. He sees working there (the University Management School) the same as me doing the MBA. We compare notes. The impact on the company is incredible. They are getting two different people.

I have never run any of the changes out on the company as experiments. I have always done what at the time seemed to me, the collective me, what has appeared to be the right thing at the time. Total conviction. We are into areas here—the learning company and the quality management system—they overlap. There's much more, I guess it's culture change. I'm having to do a lot more conscious pushing of it.

It is not like structural change where I can say we'll reorganize that way. That's a physical thing. You move people round the building. But this is all pervasive. I do find myself in the role of not allowing general managers to stem the process and be constrained by what we used to do, or even the limit of what they're prepared to do. A lot of it is textbooky stuff. Like a quality management system being a step to TQM. You can't use any words around quality now that aren't completely hackneyed and done to death.

We are starting to change things. I don't see it as experiment, but it's certainly early. The judges are out, but, in a sense, the judges never come in because, as soon as anything appears to be going off balance, you start to change it.

To survive we've got to remain flexible. I know everybody's saying it, and I believe it. If you look at what we've done with the company in the last 3 years. We've changed and I'm always thinking about the next change, which I float across people and they just pale. That's the bit I enjoy and that's my role more than anything.

There is a strong link here between organizational and personal transformation. For example, Richard speaks of the company, 'getting two different people'. What are the possible sources of these transformations?

One clue from this story is to do with language and conceptual thinking. Richard acquired a new language and a different way of thinking from his MBA experience. This has changed the way he thinks and talks about the company. For example, when asked where he got the term 'learning company' from, he says:

> I've hijacked it. Well, I've read what other people are writing—some of it—about learning companies. It's a useful banner to give people. If I use it often enough, it actually picks up all that we want to do around the quality initiative and teaching and learning generally.

Perhaps this really is the virtual company—you start to use the words and the reality follows?

> But I actually think I can demonstrate it internally. In the last three years, we have done a lot of learning and brought down a lot of barriers. The company was fairly arrogant and it's now going into very meaningful partnerships with both educational and business partners. And we're clearly seeing the benefits of that approach.
>
> In terms of the quality initiative, we are going to have to break out of some bad habits. I co-presented on all of the QA sessions and it was a great opportunity because I saw everybody in very small groups for a day and I'm almost inclined to engineer something like it every year. At the end, when people were asked what they'd liked or what surprised them, two lots of people said, 'we were surprised to see you here'. That surprised me, but it was good. I'm using the learning company thing and, maybe because of its catering legacy, one of our core competencies is digging ourselves out of holes, but, unfortunately, we have never learned how to stop digging holes. There is this element of succeeding being having come out of a hole, but we just go and dig another one. So, the learning company is reminding people that we have to get better at these things—get better at laying the tarmac flat to start with.
>
> If you synthesize what most people define as the learning company in terms of the ability, literally, to change oneself on the basis of what has happened and adapt to make sure these things don't happen again. It's useful to have it in your mind.

Learning new things, breaking old habits—the learning company label looks a good fit. It seems important to give things a name (a possible explanation for the fads and fashion for which management theory is often criticized). So, where does Richard get his new ideas, words, concepts?

> I think that's the biggest thing the MBA did for me, to start me reading again. Now I have several books on the go at once. The problem I have now is keeping up. At the moment it's gone off a bit and that's mainly because (the latest) Tom Peters is pretty turgid. I just read through Senge. I found it fascinating. You get fired up by a particular case study or a particular idea and you use it for a while. Then you drop it off, but it's still there. This idea, this tension business is a very good concept.

Does theory help him to depersonalize problems?

> I'm sure that's right. You do actually start to see the process rather than the content. And that's what it's all about. It's about focusing on the

process when it's so easy to blame the people. The number of times I find myself using that.

In a visual demonstration of his learning in terms of conceptual thinking and language, Richard has created a model to depict the transformation of Fretwell Downing from the *technical* to the *learning* company (Figure 3.2).

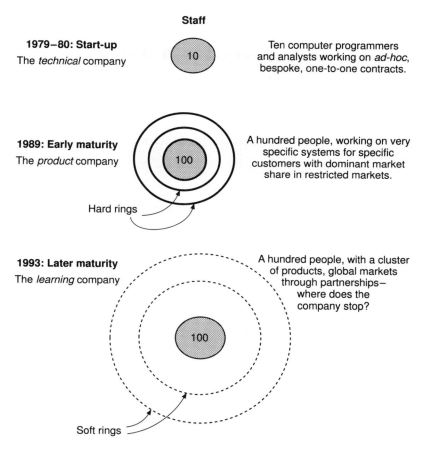

Staff

1979–80: Start-up
The *technical* company
10

Ten computer programmers and analysts working on *ad-hoc*, bespoke, one-to-one contracts.

1989: Early maturity
The *product* company
100

A hundred people, working on very specific systems for specific customers with dominant market share in restricted markets.

Hard rings

1993: Later maturity
The *learning* company
100

A hundred people, with a cluster of products, global markets through partnerships—where does the company stop?

Soft rings

Figure 3.2   The transformations of Fretwell Downing

And now?

Richard's ability to think about the development of the company in this way marks the end of this particular story.

Picking up from his discovery about the importance of the *process*—the *how* of learning—can you answer the following questions, first of all about Fretwell Downing and then for your company?

Application 5: Next steps

1. What's the picture you get of *how* people learn at Fretwell Downing?

Are there lots of ways of learning or just a few?	Lots ☐	Few ☐
Is it on- and off-job?	Yes ☐	No ☐
Is knowledge and expertise valued?	Yes ☐	No ☐
Is learning valued?	Yes ☐	No ☐
Is there an expectation that people will learn from each other?	Yes ☐	No ☐
Are all people—whatever their job—expected to learn?	Yes ☐	No ☐
Is there evidence that the top people are learning and changing?	Yes ☐	No ☐
Is there a link between learning and action?	Yes ☐	No ☐
Is there a link between action and learning?	Yes ☐	No ☐
Do people take time out for reflection?	Yes ☐	No ☐
Does the company learn from other organizations?	Yes ☐	No ☐
Are people encouraged to experiment?	Yes ☐	No ☐

2. Now try the same questions for how people learn in *your* organization

Are there lots of ways of learning or just a few?	Lots ☐	Few ☐
Is it on- and off-job?	Yes ☐	No ☐
Is knowledge and expertise valued?	Yes ☐	No ☐
Is learning valued?	Yes ☐	No ☐
Is there an expectation that people will learn from each other?	Yes ☐	No ☐
Are all people—whatever their job—expected to learn?	Yes ☐	No ☐
Is there evidence that the top people are learning and changing?	Yes ☐	No ☐
Is there a link between learning and action?	Yes ☐	No ☐
Is there a link between action and learning?	Yes ☐	No ☐
Do people take time out for reflection?	Yes ☐	No ☐
Does the company learn from other organizations?	Yes ☐	No ☐
Are people encouraged to experiment?	Yes ☐	No ☐

3. How do you and your company match up?

_____

_____

_____

4. What could you do to improve or transform things in your company?

_____

_____

_____

In *learning process* terms it is vital to know:

- *How* you learn in your company
- *How* people learn in other companies
- *How* you can do better.

Finally ...

Although Fretwell Downing has only about 100 staff, it has some characteristics of the 'bigger' company. The nature of product and the market requires a wide perspective and a worldwide orientation. As we have hinted earlier, though hardly originally, small is often beautiful when it comes to learning companies. Small companies, especially when they are young, often find it easier to learn (providing the right attitudes are there at the top), with individual learning being rapidly passed on and with the whole company meeting and moving as one.

In this chapter, we chose a small company in which to look at the issues involved in linking individual and organizational learning—one of the critical challenges for any would-be learning company. In this particular example, the individual is the managing director, and he is in a good position to put his personal learning into practice. However, while linking the learning of the MD with the organization is a good place to make a start, it is clearly a mistake to leave the MD to do all the learning for the organization. The learning of all the people who make up the company needs to be harnessed for the benefit of the whole.

It may also be argued that developing learning in the smaller company is easier than in the multinational. This may well be so, but the lessons from Fretwell Downing might revitalize much bigger cousins. As a company gets bigger and older, and perhaps especially if it achieves pre-eminence in a particular business, it seems to get harder to learn. Size alone is a problem—how can a company of 70 000 people or more do 'joined-up thinking' and learn together? As Marvin Weisbord has said, we shouldn't give up on this too easily. If we get 50 000 people into a stadium to be part of a concert, perhaps it shouldn't be beyond our wit to devise ways and means in the big company. Information technology offers one obvious channel, but there are lots of others. Chapter 5 picks up this challenge and looks at learning—or not—in the big company.

References

Pascale, R. (1990) *Managing on the Edge: How successful companies use conflict to stay ahead*, Penguin, Harmondsworth, Middlesex

Schon, D. A. (1971) *Beyond the Stable State*, Random House, New York

4 The company as a developing being

> ... companies collectively constitute a sentient, intelligent, non-human species at a relatively early stage in its evolution.
>
> (Lloyd, 1990, p. xii)

> A natural biological *organism* can be regarded as a model for a social *organization* provided one very great difference is not forgotten: the members of a social organization are independent human beings and not cells in a biological structure ... It is ... possible to imagine an 'adult' form of social organization in which all the members strive out of their own insight and conviction towards a *jointly agreed objective* ... a social organization is always 'on the way' from a given past to its own future.
>
> (Lievegoed, 1973, pp. 42–4)

In Chapter 3, we saw how the learning of a managing director led to a spread of learning throughout the company—a virtuous cycle. However, given the dominance of the owner in many small companies, a less desirable cycle may come about—if the owner doesn't learn, nobody else does.

The limits to learning in many small companies are effectively set by the style of the owner and the key managers. The more the owner sees the possibilities for their own learning, the more they are likely to create learning opportunities for others. In this chapter, we explore the notion of the company as a developing entity, with a past, a present and a future, and which is itself part of an evolving 'species'. A four-stage model of the small company shows that the owner may move towards a more facilitating role, becoming less concerned with managing or directing and more concerned with the learning of the company as a whole, developing being.

In adopting a biological metaphor as a way of understanding the development of small companies, illustrated by case extracts from owner managed companies, this chapter owes much to joint work with Ian Anderson, then Managing Director of the David Hall Partnership. This research focused on the applicability of learning organization ideas in small- and medium-sized enterprises (SMEs) and was supported by Barnsley and Doncaster and Rotherham Training and Enterprise Councils (TECs).

The *small* learning company

If companies are a species, then small companies—of 10, 20, 50 or 150 people—are the dominant life form. As Figure 4.1 shows, they are a key component of the European economy.

Table 4.1   Companies by size in the European Community (1988)

Size by employees	Number of enterprises (%)	Employment Share (%)
Micro (1–9)	92.1	29.8
Small and medium (10–500)	7.8	41.3
Large (500+)	0.1	28.9

(*Source*: Eurostat 1992, in Clarke and Monkhouse, 1994, p. 213)

One analysis of the German *Mittelstands* suggests that:

> About 50 per cent of our GNP comes from these companies ... they employ 65 per cent of employees and take about 86 per cent of apprentices.... Labour relations are normally much better and more individualised than in the large corporations. In the German machine-building industry, which is the largest export branch, the average size of the company is 300 employees, but the average export rate is between 60 per cent and 65 per cent. That means a typical 300 employee company, with the owner still as chief executive officer at the top, travelling all over the world, selling his machines, even if he comes from a small villlage in the provinces of Germany, is the model that is successful.
> (Weiss, 1992, quoted by Clarke and Monkhouse, 1994, p. 16)

While they do not dominate economies, aggregate employment figures or financial gossip columns, small companies do create the most new jobs, contribute greatly to exports and GNP, stabilize local communities and—crucial to our argument here—are potentially more flexible, adaptable and able to learn faster than their larger cousins. Moreover the larger companies are becoming smaller. In 1984, Unilever employed 90 000 people in the UK, but, by 1994, this was down to as few as 13 000—*one seventh* of the number just 10 years before—yet turnover was up more than 300 per cent. (Goyder, 1994, p. xi)

Defining 'small', the Bolton Report said:

> First, in economic terms, a small firm is one that has a relatively small share of its market. Secondly, an essential charactereristic of

a small firm is that it is managed by its owners or part-owners in a personalised way, and not through the medium of a formalised management structure. Thirdly, it is also independent in the sense that it does not form part of a larger enterprise and that the owner-managers should be free from outside control in taking their principal decisions.

(Bolton, 1971, p. 1)

The companies in the research sample on which this chapter is based fulfilled the criteria of *size*—being between 50 and 200 employees; *independence*—they were not subsidiaries of larger groups; and being *owner-managed*. Additionally, they demonstrated an interest in learning and development, both of individuals and of the company as a whole.

In case this last point goes unremarked, several studies have confirmed that many small firms do *not* show this interest. Typically, small companies stay small, with owners choosing autonomy and independence over growth and development. Whether this stems from limited horizons, a lack of confidence or from positive choices, such businesses are often reluctant to admit or use outside expertise and are very sceptical about the value of existing management training and development services to small businesses. (National Small Firms Policy and Research Conference, 1993) Current Government strategy, following pioneer programmes such as Business Growth Training, is to encourage companies to become 'Investors in People' and to equip their people with National Vocational Qualifications (NVQs). These schemes have some merit, particularly in giving impetus to consideration of the link between individual and organizational learning.

However, in addition to the reservations expressed in Chapter 2, there is a danger of proliferating initiatives. Too many unrelated schemes add to the fragmentation of the times. How can the various quality improvement and training initiatives be integrated? What is the vision for the whole organization? These are major challenges for the smaller, as well as the larger, company.

What does it mean to talk about companies as if they were members of a species? Or to talk of companies as living organisms following a development path in pursuit of a goal? Organizational biography work is a way of working with companies from this standpoint. We look at some of these ideas before developing a stage model of small company development. The chapter concludes by asking whether larger companies can learn from the example of smaller members of the species.

The company as a developing organism

From this perspective organizations are in a dynamic process of becoming, and of *being* only in transition. The biographical metaphor, with its births and deaths, ages and stages, events, periods and themes, lends itself well to this perspective. Organizations are formed from three forces:

- *ideas*   the visions and images that founders seek to realize and which are passed on to succeeding generations to recreate;
- *phase*   the life stage of the company—infant, pioneer, rational, overripe bureaucracy, dying;
- *era*   the economic, social, political and cultural context.

(Pedler, Burgoyne and Boydell, 1991, pp. 3 and 4)

Approaches to the study of organizations can be seen to favour one or other of these forces. For example, *organizational development* practitioners tend to stress the importance of having the right ideas and values as expressed in 'vision driven by empowering leadership'. *Organizational ecologists* eschew the study of single organizations for studies of population survival rates in particular environments. The agential assumptions of the former—that organizations control their own destinies and can plot their future course—are confronted here by more deterministic ones, which give primacy to environments and contextual forces. For the latter, the actions of individual companies are inconsequential and of little interest. *Organizational biography* focuses on the life of the individual organization over time, and occupies intermediate ground between the agential and the deterministic. Those who have taken this perspective include Greiner (1972), Lievegoed (1973) and Adizes (1988), although a related notion, the 'lifecycle model', has been described by Porter as the 'grandfather' of all business models (1980, p. 157).

Organizational biography builds on the organism metaphor and sees companies as living systems, exchanging with a wider environment to satisfy their needs. Related metaphors, include those of organizations as 'cultures', 'brains', 'flux and transformation' (Morgan, 1986). Salama (1992) goes beyond 'culture' and uses the term *personalities*—'every company must be understood as an individual with its own idiosyncracies'. This takes us beyond organism to the metaphor of 'person' or 'living being' with a unique life forged from inheritance, circumstances and some free will to make decisions at various times.

This might feel a bit odd, but we do think of and refer to our organizations as living and changing, as learning or not learning. For example, two owners describe their companies:

It's like a tree that's been grafted upon, an old tree that has been given a new lease of life, shrugging off the old stuff and growing new foliage.

(Peter Keary, Elton Hotel)

Growth oriented ... quality, supporting, helping, dependable, sound, reliable ... here for you to depend on for years to come.

(Rob Drohan, ACE)

Living, and learning   How is it that some people grow in stature and wisdom, while others never live up to early promise? How do some companies, vibrant and dynamic in youth, become dull and lose their way while others find creative ways to renew their energy and purpose?

I took over as MD at a time when the company needed to change. It had grown rapidly on one particular market sector and was skewed around that. I got to the point where I couldn't learn anything else, anything fundamental. It was going to be incremental learning only and it was necessary to break out. Until then the culture of the company was basically that you either learned on the job or you relied on bringing in new people. We were in a position in those first 6 to 8 years of meteoric growth where we could do that.

(Richard Plumb, Fretwell Downing)

We also talk of the company growing old:

All these initiatives that we get involved in—of management training, Investors In People, quality and so on—only replicate what we did as a matter of common sense when we were a very small company. We didn't think about it then, we were just such a close-knit team, communication was 100% efficient, we were always conscious of the need to do the job right, people just developed on the job, although even in those days people went to night school or on day release if there was something that was needed. You never needed prompting ...

During the middle years we did lose that. It's taken conscious effort, conscious thought to bring that back into what is now a larger business. It's a bit ironic that so much effort has to go into doing something that we once found easy!

(Rob Drohan, ACE)

In the early days, when they were young, learning wasn't a problem for either of these companies. One imported knowledge in the shape of able new people; the other's small, close-knit staff group shared such a common understanding that all did what was needful without prompting. For both companies, however, a time came when these strategies were no longer adequate and they had to undertake deliberate learning strategies.

Before we move on to the next point, think about your company in this respect.

Application 6: Ages and stages

1. Thinking of your company, and ignoring for the moment its actual chronological age, which of the following would you say best characterized its current stage of development?

Infant ☐

Toddler ☐

Child ☐

Adolescent ☐

Suspended adolescent ☐

Young adult ☐

Adult ☐

Mature adult ☐

Middle-aged ☐

Old ☐

2. Now, think of the company as it was *five years ago*, what stage was it at then?

_____

3. Now, imagine the company *five years from now*, what stage will it have reached by then?

_____

4. Would you say that your company was developing or would you say that it was just putting on years?

_____

Life and death

If there is life and a lifecycle, then there must also be death. Many infant companies are short-lived, with, typically, 40 per cent not surviving their first year. To survive at all, an organization needs a reason for being beyond the idea of the founder. It must have users who want the service or product, a business potential, a market. The small pioneer organization that has this demand for its services is often a busy, active place, full of learning. The learning, so to speak, takes place naturally.

If many infant companies do not survive, many long-lived institutions appear to lose the capacity to learn. The danger to learning lies beyond the pioneer stage, especially when specialist roles and departments begin to appear, functions are separated—when we start 'doing things properly'. People, divided from each other by boundaries of function, status, professional training and so on, fragment and cease to connect. The learning by individuals throughout the company remains as local knowledge. We can reach the situation described earlier where the company cannot learn what everybody in it knows!

Organizational ecologists have brought to our attention the traumas of organizational conception, gestation, birth and death (Kimberly and Miles, 1980). Organizational death does not figure greatly in the theories of organization development, which may account, in part, for their tendency to 'look on the bright side', but contemporary evidence suggests that the ecologists' assumption about the species is now the likely fate, sooner or later, of all companies. Pascale notes that:

> Of the corporations in the Fortune 500 rankings five years ago, 143 are missing today. (By comparison, in the 25 years, 1955 to 1980, only 238 dropped out.)
>
> (1991, pp. 11–17)

So, this appears to be an accelerating trend. Commenting on Peters and Waterman's 1982 sample of 'excellent' companies, Pascale notes further that, 'Only five years after the book's publication, two thirds of the companies studied had slipped from the pinnacle'. Findings like these may partly explain an upsurge of interest in organizational learning—perhaps corporate learning can stave off the inevitable?

It has been suggested that organizations, as larger-than-life structures that can continue for generations, act as a defence against the natural anxieties of being human and mortal. However, an acknowledgement of the eventual likelihood of organizational death may offer greater maturity and the 'sculpted creativity' of later life (Jaques, 1970, pp. 38–63). The denial of death perhaps constitutes an important aspect of the 'shadow side' of organizational life:

> Jung's work shows that the repressed shadow of organisation acts as a reservoir not only of forces that are unwanted and hence repressed but of forces that have been lost or undervalued. By recognising and coming to grips with the resources of this reservoir, Jungian organisation theorists are at one in suggesting

that we can tap new sources of energy and creativity and make our institutions much more human, vibrant, and morally responsive and responsible than they are now.

(Morgan, 1986, p. 225)

Sometimes organizations do outlast their useful lives and, in continuing to exist, deny the new. Facing up to this and, with care and proper ceremony, choosing the right time to make a good end, can release new life and energy. In Chapter 9 we tell the story of Sheffield's Manor Employment Project, founded in 1980, to create small businesses with local people, which voted, after a long struggle, to end itself in 1987, to be replaced by MaTReC (Manor Training and Resources Centre), the new training and educational aims of which better fitted the needs of the times.

Developmental management

To the extent that we can see the company as a dynamic being with a lifecycle, we can talk about its development over time. Although every organization is unique, meeting particular problems and circumstances, it is possible to talk about predictable questions that occur at predictable times. For example, the early creative pioneer phase often ends in a crisis of leadership, where the young company—full of the founders' drive and vision—struggles when they leave, retire or lose their way.

In this view, the development of a company takes place via a progression of phases that are irreversible. Development is discontinuous. An old pattern is broken by the crisis and a new one forms over time, and involves qualitative transformation. Each succeeding phase is different in quality from the old and is characterized by a different principle. (Greiner, 1972; Lievegoed, 1973)

This implies conscious, developmental management. The company is seen as a continuous system over time with a past, a present and a future. There is learning to be had from the past, perhaps most importantly that to do with organizational values and identity. Development requires a present state of readiness to take the next step and an optimistic future orientation to provide vision and courage. To manage developmentally means recognizing where the company is in terms of the developmental sequence, recognizing the nature of the crisis when it comes, and seeing the opportunities to develop inherent in that crisis. In 1983, a study of chief executive officers in the USA showed that those with most awareness of past events also looked further into the future (Kouzes and Posner, 1987, p. 95). And in the small businesses:

> What we've done from the early days is to estimate the size of the market we were working in, decide what market share we wanted and what the implications were for us ... trying to develop a vision of where we would be in five years' time ... I only got involved because I was aware this business had potential. This was never going to remain a two man business.
>
> (Rob Drohan, ACE)

Of course, in thinking about companies as living beings, we must never forget that we are using a particular lens or metaphor. Like any other single view, this is a limited one that gives special significance to the individual, to the unique and special case. Its strength comes from the reflective *inside* story that biography work can offer and the generation of new ideas and meanings to help the company with its current concerns and future direction.

Mapping the company's biography—ages, stages and phases

Large companies can and do spend huge amounts on change programmes that appear to have very little impact. Often, change programmes *don't* produce change! Changes tend only to have lasting effects when they address an underlying need in the company. A developmental perspective always has an eye on what is to be achieved in the longer term. From this perspective, any change is judged not only against the question 'Does this help us deal with our current problems?', but also 'Does this help us take *our next step* as a company?'

Companies can be seen as developing in phases, each of which is appropriate to start with but becomes less so as time goes on. Many companies go through:

- a free-form, *infant* phase (when they first start)
- a more autocratic, *pioneer* phase (where the founder(s) dominates)
- a more bureaucratic, *rational* phase (where rational management systems replace the personal, idiosyncratic control of the founder)
- a more democratic, *integrated* phase (where the systems are loosened up, people are developed and trusted to work on their own initiative, partnership with others and so on).

A way of using this idea is to sketch the phases you see in the biography of your company, and choose your own names to give to them. In Figure 4.1, we have added some phases to those listed above to show examples of where companies lost their sense of purpose, died or radically changed in character.

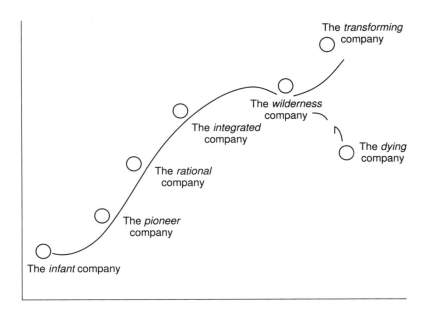

Figure 4.1 Some phases of organizational biography
(*Source:* Pedler, Burgoyne and Boydell, 1991, p. 36)

Of course, this is too simple. Real companies are unique, more complex and no one company conforms to any one type. In turbulent times, a company's ability to experiment and change appropriately is vital—this is part of what it means to be a learning company. But, like some people, some companies always want to try something different. Diversifications, new systems, new products, new markets, fads and fashions often turn out to be mistakes. Some of this may be due to a failure to take a long view—a view of the company as a being in the process of becoming, with a past, a present and a future.

If the study of American chief executives mentioned above is right, being able to learn from the company's past, to reflect on and honour that history, is an important step in moving from the present into the future. Before we move on, think about your company's past biography.

Application 7: Key learning events in the company's biography

1. List some of the events in the past that have made your company the organization it is today. If you have been with the company for less than five years, you could talk to some of the 'older hands' at this point. Pick out five or six *key learning events* (KLEs)—learning experiences that have had an important effect on the company.

1. _____

2. _____

3. _____

4. _____

5. _____

6. _____

2. Mark these on a graph to form a 'lifeline' (see the following example). Because KLEs affect the development of the company, they often appear as turning points for declines or rises in fortune.

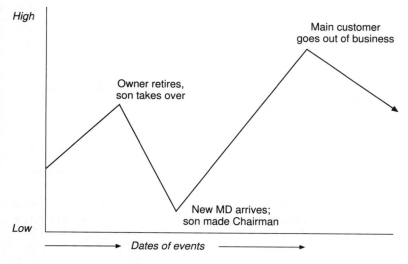

Figure 4.2   The company lifeline

What does *your* company's lifeline look like?

3. Now, looking at the KLEs you have identified for your company, can you say for each one:

	KLE 1	KLE 2	KLE 3	KLE 4	KLE 5	KLE 6
What happened?						
What sort of change was involved?						
What difference did this make?						
What was learned of lasting value, that is, which lives on now in the company?						

4. Think about the KLEs in the life of your company.

How have these shaped the character or personality of your company as it is today?

_____

_____

_____

Have there been one or two particularly influential events that have strongly determined the direction of the company from then on?

_____

_____

_____

If one or more of these events had not happened, can you imagine how things could have been different? What alternative life path might the company have followed if these events had not taken place?

_____

_____

_____

Like people, companies are partly a product of what has happened to them—their past decisions and choices and those things that just happen over which relatively little choice was exercised.

In the lifeline example given, one of the KLEs was a sort of choice (although the implications had *not* been planned for), one was a clear decision and the third was just something that happened and the company had to adjust and learn from it afterwards.

Good planning and decision making can 'save' us from some KLEs we would rather do without, but, ironically, we often learn most from those that just happen without our being prepared for them.

Can we sketch out a standard development model that applies to all small companies?

A four-stage model of company development

Much of what we've said about developmental management applies to all companies. However, in smaller companies, often the first and last factor of importance to note is the power and centrality of the owner. So normal as to be easily overlooked, it is clear that, for most such companies, their destiny, and therefore their biography, is bound up inextricably with that of their owners. This is so for many reasons—it is *their* company, they own it; they are also the founders, holders and champions of the original idea. Add to these a long association and a commitment of most of their waking hours, and the owner has often become synonymous with the company. Frequently, another factor—personality—is in play. These are often creative, driven and 'big' people who have become so identified with the company that it is a corporate extension of their personality. Several of these explanations are often found in combination, and it is more usual than not to find small companies managed and directed by these powerful figures.

This leads us to an important finding, namely that the personal development of the owner and the business development of the company are often closely linked. Because of their dominance, owners' knowledge, skills, opinions and beliefs, prides and prejudices are likely to be strongly imprinted on the collective body. The limits to their knowledge and skill are likely to be those of the whole unless they can achieve the personal security to get beyond simple dominance and to facilitate the development of all the people in the company as a whole.

From owner-operator to owner-developer
Building on the biographical approach, it is possible to create a four-stage model of small company development that shows

a changing role and purpose for the owner. Following the biography approach outlined earlier, these are:

1. Owner-operated
2. Owner-managed
3. Owner-directed
4. Owner-developed.

We illustrate this model with a case study of Weldrick, a retail pharmacy chain in South Yorkshire, before taking a closer look at these stages of development to reveal some distinctive characteristics of the organization and the owner's role.

CASE: Weldrick

Weldrick, a retail pharmacy chain of 22 shops, warehouse and a 1993 turnover of £12 million, is the creation of owner, Mr Ron Alcock. Business is in his family background—his grandmother, an entrepreneur and shopkeeper, was an important early influence. He has a strong entrepreneurial drive, which he sees as unusual in pharmacists, and is dominant in the business, displaying an impressive grasp of both strategy and detail.

History and growth

> I qualified in 1964 and opened my first business on April Fools Day 1967—the takings were £16 and 4 pence and I dispensed 22 scripts. On 29th November 1973, I bought H. I. Weldrick and at that time had about six branches.

Growth has been rapid and smooth, with turnover rising year on year. There have been plateaux, as in 1986/7 when a change in the law meant that NHS contracts were only awarded to pharmacies more than a mile apart. This slowed growth and put up the price of pharmacies because of the guaranteed markets.

> ... after 1986/7, I decided that the business had got big enough that we actually needed some stronger management ... We had reached a stage where I couldn't do everything ... formally training people, getting better calibre people and being better organized. After saying all this, I must say that I made more profit in 1975 than I do now—it all goes on staff and the central office overheads.

Given the right people and his close monitoring of performance all the time, the handing over of these responsibilities was 'relatively painless'. A few mistakes were made and two of the people appointed did not meet expectations. The business clearly changed in this period, with the delegation of management functions, a more ambitious vision and a five-year strategic plan:

> A key change was the creation of a strategic plan ... and sticking to it, which has had quite an impact on the direction and helped everyone to focus on what they're doing ... we review it every three months, but

the people who formed it meet weekly and discuss parts of it all the time.

The Retail Director, previously a shop manager, is now responsible for profitability and, while Mr Alcock shows some willingness to allow new people to influence the purpose and direction, he retains a firm grip. As well as managing strategically, he goes on more professional refresher courses than anyone else and still works in the branches, dispensing, once a week:

> to keep in touch and to keep my hand in for my own satisfaction ... I do like pharmacy and I do like meeting my customers, and the only way of getting the marketing right and to monitor the situation is to be there. And monitor with a capital M—that was a New Year's Resolution about two years ago and it's still top of the list.

Monitoring on the inside

Weldrick is managed by monthly returns from branches, which are turned into a central computer report. Each manager has targets for the year and gets a detailed monthly report with 'league tables' on their branch performance on key indicators, such as turnover, prescriptions, retail sales, staff costs and stock against the other branches. If targets are met, bonuses for managers and staff are payable. Computerization will soon link bonuses to profitability in branches.

All stock must be ordered from the warehouse to maximize control and bulk buying. Geographical spread means there is little competition between branches. A 'branch of the month' award recognizes special achievements. The managers' meetings have become livelier of late, with the consultant's help, and Mr Alcock contrasts them with earlier occasions when he did all the talking. Feedback of information to managers is on a need-to-know basis and is limited to branch operations. Is there a case for involving managers more in thinking about the company as a whole?

> They are a super team and they do try to benefit the company as a whole ... for example, a new warehouse computer has been letting us down, and they've really helped in every way, filling in yellow cards to report any faults, they've helped us enormously ... but you must remember that a pharmacist is an academic and very few of them are business-aware. We have all on to make them business-minded in the shop never mind as a group ... I think really ... they'd drown if we tried to make them too involved.

The character of the business:

> ... is a good, solid family business rather than a monster out of control or an empire where we have ways of making you do things. We get people to respond far better that way, and I suppose in a strange sort of way I think of the staff in the same way as my family.

Monitoring on the outside

Keeping in touch with the outside world is one of Mr Alcock's key roles. He searches all trade journals and notes product developments, national and international trends, legislative changes and so on.

> If I delegated it I would always fear something was missed … and it keeps me in touch at the same time … more than anybody else. I study all planning applications to every council where we have branches and go through them for surgeries opening or moving, change of use notices, nursing homes, etc … I just sleep better doing it personally.

Mr Alcock also sits on a pharmaceutical subcommittee of the local Family Health Service Association (FHSA), which coordinates local primary health care. This keeps him in touch with all new, local health care developments and one effect of this is that Weldricks' shop displays are coordinated with the FHSA's theme of the month—keeping warm, breast feeding, stopping smoking and so on.

Learning and experiment

Does the company learn from what others do? Mr Alcock does not think other chains have much to offer, but cites learning from Boots. When Boots set up a controlled unit dispensing system of drugs for nursing homes, all Weldrick's nursing homes were offered a similar, free system.

Weldrick is more interested in experimenting with new ideas. A lockable display shelving system has been patented for items the sale of which must be supervised by the pharmacist. As a result, several articles have appeared in national magazines featuring the company. Postal dispensing is a recent innovation and prescriptions can even be faxed in.

On the training front, there are induction programmes and operations manuals for both managers and shop staff. Pharmacists, and sometimes other staff, are encouraged to update their product knowledge by attending seminars. The company has an in-house training facility with distance learning opportunities and has done management training under the various grant schemes.

How does Mr Alcock evaluate this training effort? Staff turnover has reduced almost to zero and staff respond enthusiastically, for example to the medical counter assistants course, where they seem to retain the knowledge afterwards and take pressure off the pharmacists.

The owner's learning experiences are often a guide to the attitude to the company's learning climate. Mr Alcock cites the value of an Institute of Directors Diploma, but he has a lot of other good learning habits:

> I learned a lot from the course … I was aware of a lot but it sharpened my awareness and made me use it … and the workshops were fantastic. I read a lot—the *Director, Management Today* … I've not really had a mentor. I suppose I've mentored myself through reading. I talk now with

Marshall (the Retail Director) and I've always talked a lot with my wife about the business. And going right back, my grandmother ... she was a very organised person and I learned a lot from her about being organised, having things in the right places and being tidy ... and from Ian (a consultant) as well ... he's come up with some ideas ... listening to Ian and reading his reports has helped a great deal.

1987 marked the beginnings of the use of outside consultants. Mr Alcock had always felt a need for outside knowledge, but had never thought it cost-effective until he was able to get a grant. Now he would do it without a grant because of the benefits he has experienced.

The future
The vision of the future is to 'dominate retail pharmacy in South Yorkshire' and continue expanding while staying tight-knit. Electronic point of sale (EPOS) capability in all branches will facilitate better stock control, merchandising, security and accounting and also help to respond more rapidly to changes. Other developments include an expansion of 'own label' products, a health shop, employing a marketing person and a representative for nursing homes and factories.

With the help of consultants, Weldrick is becoming an 'Investor in People' and responsibility for training and development will be delegated to the shops. In future, the people employed by Weldrick will be more highly qualified and of a higher standard. Postgraduate education for pharmacists is becoming compulsory.

Mr Alcock forsees great business opportunities in the Government's plan to unload the NHS and doctors by increasing services from pharmacies. A new payment system will reward performance on specific services, such as establishing private consultation areas in pharmacies, from each pharmacy handling patients' medical records to offering house deliveries and for staff going on refresher courses and other services in areas of work hitherto part of the GP's preserve, such as initial diagnosis of diabetes, cholesterol testing, pregnancy testing and dietary advice.

On succession, he is ready to step back and be chairman, but he does not intend to retire—it is not a word in his vocabulary:

Now I've got to this stage in life ... I would gladly be paid to keep out of the way as long as I had all the facts ... so I could still monitor the situation! When the information I can get from the computer is exactly what I want, then I will be content to step back.

A four-stage model of small company development

The Weldrick case is unique, but it is also typical in many respects of the formation, development and character of many small businesses. As discussed earlier, here is a classic example of the centrality of the owner, which affects *all* aspects of the company as a developing being—its personality, how it came to be this way, what it may become and how it learns or not.

While this model applies specifically to such small companies, there are plenty of examples of very large concerns, including multinationals, that are dominated by their owners or leaders. Although this pattern was far more marked in the past, current examples include Rupert Murdoch's News Corporation, Richard Branson's Virgin and Anita Roddick's The Body Shop.

Stage 1: The owner-operated company

At this early stage, the company has been brought into being by the founder, who is the main, or even the only, worker. He or she does everything from origination of the order to delivery of finished product or service (see Figure 4.3). Systems are personal, idiosyncratic and may be good or bad. What drives the company is the personal vision and energy of the owner-founder. People are busy, work long hours and learn quickly.

In the Weldrick case Mr Alcock started in this mode and continued in some aspects of it for some time. For example, he used to do all the shop fitting and only gave this up when he owned some dozen branches.

Owner finds customers, creates and delivers product or service, does books, etc.

Figure 4.3   Stage 1: Owner-operated—owner as operator

Stage 2: The owner-managed company

In the second stage—the owner-managed company—much more rationality has entered the organization. Personal energy and vision are no longer sufficient and the company brings in professional expertise, trained staff and management systems, sometimes as a result of a crisis caused when the founder has retired, withdrawn or otherwise lessened in influence.

Now there a sense of functional management with different people specializing in production, marketing, design and so on (see Figure 4.4). The owner is likely to be the main or only manager, a bit less 'hands-on' than before, not doing everything but coordinating the work of the others. They continue to make all the important decisions.

Figure 4.4   Stage 2: Owner-managed—owner as manager

As a pharmacist and shopowner, Mr Alcock was in this mode more or less from the beginning. The managerial content of his work grew over time until he couldn't handle it all and he began to move into stage 3. However, it is worth noticing that, even now, not only does he retain key aspects of managing, but he still dispenses and serves customers, retaining some of the owner-operator.

Stage 3: The owner-directed company
At the third stage, the owner ceases to be the only or main manager and other people grow into key managerial roles. They may become directors or partners and now form a management team that makes collective decisions. While the power of the owner, as chairman, is still dominant, there is more debate and even disagreement.

The main role of the owner as director is two-fold: looking in and looking out (see Figure 4.5). They monitor the internal operations of the company to make sure that policy is reflected in operations and that feedback from operations modifies policy appropriately, as well as monitoring the outside world for changes in the market, competitor actions, legislative or government policy trends and so on. The director is the 'business brain', linking the inner world of the company with the outer environment (Garratt, 1987).

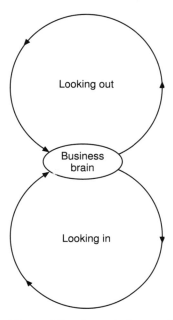

Figure 4.5   Stage 3: Owner-directed—owner as director

By now, the company may have begun to establish some management or team development as well as essential operative training. The company as a whole learns from spotting internal operating variations from plan and adjusting, and by developing new policy as a result of spotting outside opportunities or threats.

In the Weldrick case, this mode best fits the current situation. Mr Alcock is an indefatigable internal monitor and a vigilant environmental scanner, and this way of being at his time in life suits him well. He still keeps a tight grip on the company and can see no good reason for moving to the next stage.

Stage 4: Owner-developed company

In the most developed form of this model, the owner has stepped back further from the management, leadership and direction of the company. They now take primary responsibility for developing the organization as a learning company.

The outer and inner monitoring of environment and operations is largely done by others. These *collective*, or whole-company functions, from the previous stage are now called *policy* (for looking out) and *operations* (for looking in), as shown in Figure 4.6.

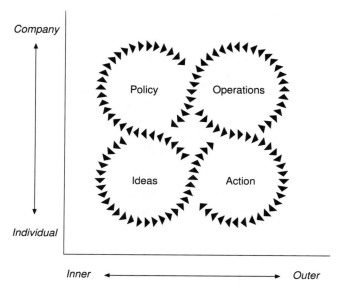

Figure 4.6   Stage 4: Owner-developer—owner as developer

At this stage, the learning of all the people in the company becomes important to the whole company's purpose and task. The two lower areas in Figure 4.6 represent the ideas and actions of *individuals*—all the individual members of the company. If a person's *ideas* flow into their *actions* and then the experience of these actions is taken back into their thinking, then the person is *learning*.

The continuous flow of energy, information and learning between *policy* and *operations* and back again is the *collective*, or corporate, learning cycle.

The continuous flow of energy, information and learning between *ideas* and *action*, and vice versa, is the *individual*, or personal, learning cycle.

The prime purpose of the owner as developer is to facilitate both collective and individual learning in the company. A key task is to find ways of linking them together so that the company harnesses the learning of all its people and so that each person can draw on the resources of the whole in doing their work.

While we can describe quite well what the owner does as operator, manager and director, we are still learning about the role of owner as developer. The Weldrick case illustrates the first three, but the fourth must remain hypothetical. What we *can* do is ask that crucial question for all would-be learning companies, 'Why change a winning team?'.

Why change a winning team?

Given a healthy trading position, it is hard to justify tampering with a 'winning team' on the basis of an uncertain future. Yet, because it is difficult to move from comfort to discomfort, many companies do not make a move until crisis is on them. Then it can be too late.

As noted earlier, ACE Conveyor Equipment Limited found it took a 'conscious effort' to get the learning habit back. In fact, 'back' is the wrong word; we can't go back. ACE took steps to learn how to learn in their new circumstances, to make them fit for the future.

Why change a 'winning team'? Even if a company is doing well, there are still at least four reasons for making a change towards being more of a learning company:

1. the problem of succession
2. the probability of continuing rapid growth
3. the possibility of environmental change
4. the possibility of change from within.

Succession
Many small (and some larger companies) founder on the rocks of replacing the central person. In small companies, family members may often be 'groomed' to step up to maintain continuity, which is such an essential ingredient in that first requirement of survival. Because they often don't have the same drive or qualities of the founder, however, this may not be successful:

> I've seen it with those who've had businesses, and brought their children into the business ... they were comfortable, didn't perhaps have the same motivation ... thought it was easy.
>
> (Ian Byrne, Fencing Construction)

Growth— more of the same
A second possibility is that of the company growing rapidly. In such circumstances, there are increased costs from the management systems needed as a result of this growth.

Additionally, there may be a loss of vitality and energy in the extended organization—as the founder draws back or loses grip, the initial vision long exceeded. Growth may make a currently adequate operating system and structure ineffective:

> We had reached a stage where I couldn't do everything ... the business would have been out of control had we not done something—formally training people, getting better calibre people and being better organised.

> (Ron Alcock, Weldrick)

Change in the environment

It is sometimes difficult to anticipate outside changes, however good your environmental monitoring and your flexibility and adaptability. The American airline People's Express grew rapidly to become a threat to the established majors, but then failed because it got everything right *except* its judgement of the importance of computer reservations systems. The majors controlled these and strangled the dynamic upstart (Hampden-Turner, 1992). This danger can often be averted if the company is alert:

> ... obviously Boot's idea had spurred us into doing it and nursing homes, as a result of that, you got a far better product and service.

> (Ron Alcock, Weldrick)

Change from within

We tend to notice change that comes from without, but occasionally it can come from within. Directors and managers are often concerned with keeping control and this possibility is reduced by the tightness of that control. However, as a result of market forces that make skilled people less dispensable or because of training opportunities or because people become more proactive for any other reason, then they may begin to question company policies and procedures in a way that it has not experienced before.

Without entirely being aware of it, owners may encourage change from within as they seek to develop their companies in the ways we have been discussing. They often want their people to be more proactive regarding the needs of the business and the by-product of this will be to increase the influence of those people:

> I had to ease off a bit, I was running myself into the ground ...
> It's very hard for me to start delegating because it had taken me
> eight years to build the business up ... Building up a team has
> helped me to share some responsibilities ... helps solve the
> problems.
>
> (Peter Keary, Elton Hotel)

All these four possibilities, and others, may happen or not.
Beyond the specifics, it is vital to live with the notion that all
companies are dynamic, even when they are 'consolidating'.
Equally, all environments are dynamic. The company does
not and cannot stand still.

Improving or transforming?

Having decided to change your winning team for the future
benefits this may bring, there are two broad learning processes
involved.

One of these we call *improving*, and is the incremental, day-
to-day learning of how to make current systems and procedures work better. This is the 'continuous improvement' of
Total Quality Management and is what everybody in the
company should be doing all the time. When we set out to
create a learning 'attitude' or 'habit', it is this we are trying
create in the company. In Figure 4.7, we liken this to climbing
a ladder.

However, this sort of learning is not always sufficient. A
learning company has a climate of continuous learning, but it
also needs to be able to change radically when appropriate.

At certain times, it becomes apparent that we can't continue
as we are and that we need to make a discontinuous change in
the company. We call this learning process *transforming*. The
need to transform the company only happens occasionally,
which is fortunate as it is necessarily disruptive to the way we
currently do things and requires a considerable investment of
time, energy and resources:

> For me personally, having someone in from outside the business
> (a non-executive director) with the ability to say things which
> inside people would not, and to suggest changes which signifi-
> cantly alter the way the business is run, is not an easy experience
> to go through. I don't think people should go in for this lightly.
> But at the end of the day it's been great for us.
>
> (Rob Drohan, ACE)

In Figure 4.7, we liken this process to jumping ladders.

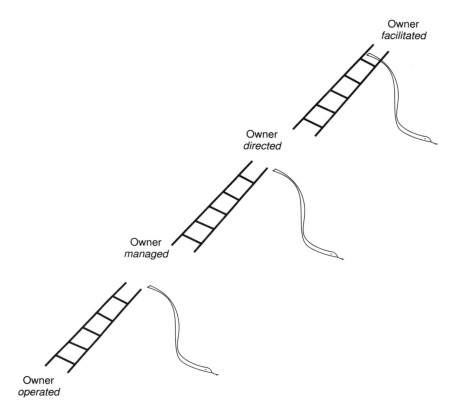

Owner
facilitated

Owner
directed

Owner
managed

Owner
operated

Figure 4.7   The snakes and ladders of small company development

The learning company climbs the ladders of development by *improving* current practice on a daily basis and is also able to *transform* itself by jumping to the next ladder when this is appropriate. Obviously, the jump from, say, owner-operator to owner-manager will not be achieved without some effort and probably some pain—of giving up on some familiar things and learning some unfamiliar things. For this reason, *transforming* often takes place when a crisis has started or is impending. The ability to use outside help and expertise is often crucial for transforming—it is hard to move into the unknown.

Not all owners want, or are able to cope with, radical change of this kind and the company remains in its current phase. This may be fine—we all know of small companies that have continued to do business in the same way for decades—but it seems the odds lessen daily. That's why the snakes are there.

What does a learning company do?

On the basis of this chapter, small companies learn from:

- *past experience* and *present performance*
- *inside* and *outside,* and
- *future plans.*

They also cultivate certain

- *habits.*

And the learning of the

- *owner* is crucial.

Learning from past experience

Is there clarity of purpose? Do people understand the idea behind the business and how has it changed?

A company learns best when there is an awareness of past events and what was learned from them, where there is a perception of development over time.

Present performance inside

Inside the organization, there is an awareness of how we learn as a company—examples of this can be given. Performance of individuals and of the company as a whole is monitored and improvement plans and projects are part of everyday life:

> People are reviewed every four months to encourage quick progression from drawing board to computer and then to take over a project and manage it. In the field teams, people go from labourer to team worker to team leader and then to supervise.
>
> (Ted Campbell, Gorseline)

There is evidence of the company learning from its staff.

Present performance outside

On the outside, the company is busy learning from all its trading partners—from customers, suppliers, from other companies—both in terms of benchmarking good practice and in spotting things to avoid:

> We are now within the top ten in the industry and seen as a larger player in the field ... We are a human face, not part of a very large firm ... you will meet us; we are not locked in an office, so we sell ourselves like this ... they get more direct access to management.
>
> (Ian Byrne, Fencing Construction)

The company understands the importance of learning partnerships with colleges, schools, other companies:

> We didn't get the theoretical training off-site, we had to learn everything inside which probably made it harder to learn. That's why I take a great interest in youth training ... I'm all for pushing

the image of the industry, trying to get youth involved and encouraging them to go to college.

(Peter Keary, Elton Hotel)

The company shows an ability and willingness to use the expertise and knowledge of outsiders, consultants and other sources and has a track record of obtaining and using grants, development schemes and so on.

Company learning habits

As part of the working routine, people in the organization take time out for reviews and reflection on their recent experience:

> We want to develop but only to change in a progressive not a revolutionary way. We have a five-year plan and we know where we are going in quite a lot of detail ... We monitor on a monthly basis and rebudget and check out strategy annually ... but every three years or so we find it necessary to sit back and say 'Where are we against where we said we were going to be?'
>
> (Rob Drohan, ACE)

The company abounds with examples of people developing and learning new skills. There is a sense of a company learning style and culture:

> I'm very lucky to have good personal staff; they all like what they're doing. This is one of our themes—we want people who want to do it rather than have got to do it.
>
> (Peter Keary, Elton Hotel)

Owner's self-awareness and learning

The owner shows considerable self-awareness and is concerned with their own personal development. They have a tendency to invest in training and development of other people in the company and also show the ability and willingness to experiment with new ideas in order to learn.

> Ever since I qualified, I've been going on post-graduate courses ... I read a lot ... I talk now with Marshall and I've always talked a lot with my wife about the business. And going right back to my grandmother .... Listening to Ian and reading his reports has helped a good deal.
>
> (Ron Alcock, Weldrick)

In a well-developed company, there is evidence of feedback and challenge to the owner, and an ability to tolerate and learn from conflict.

Learning for the future

A learning company looks ahead, beyond the immediate operating plan, and has a vision of the future—something to go for that will change the nature of the company as it is today. There is a process in place for implementing the vision, with feedback loops and pilot schemes built in for learning purposes.

> This has been one of the features of our company's development—we have had very good advice, financial, legal, taxation, consultancy. We were very wary of management consultants because of the open ended nature of the financial commitment. It was only through the managed approach of the Training Agency we felt confident to go ahead. Since then we've always done it this way, building in performance indicators, checks and balances.
>
> (Rob Drohan, ACE)

The owner has a sense of their future role in the company and, where appropriate, succession plans are in place.

Are small companies so different?

Are these ideas only relevant to the small- or medium-sized enterprise—or is there a wider validity? Small companies clearly differ from larger ones in many respects—in scope, geography, perhaps, structure, sophistication, perhaps, and complexity certainly. However, anyone who works with small companies as a helper, adviser, consultant, cannot but be struck by their human scale—you can get to know almost everyone and, over time, understand what each thinks and what concerns them. This has good and bad sides. At best, people in small enterprises can discuss important issues together, make good, quick decisions and move into action with great speed and considerable commitment. At worst, they can be miserable, mediaeval fiefdoms where brutality and ignorance reign.

But is this so different from bigger organizations or, perhaps, for *parts* of bigger organizations? Systems of communication and consultation are necessarily more representative and arms-length, but the same sense of commitment or brutality is quickly apparent to the visitor. As bigger organizations move away from the bureaucratic command and control models of managing that no longer deliver the goods and services as well as they need to, so they come to resemble more small companies or, perhaps, federations of small businesses.

References

Adizes, I. (1988) *Corporate Lifecycles*, Prentice-Hall, New Jersey
Bolton, J. (1971) *Small Firms: Report of the Committee of Enquiry on Small Firms*, Cmnd 4811, HMSO, London

Clarke, T. and Monkhouse, E. (Eds) (1994) *Rethinking the Company*, Pitman, London

Garratt, R. (1987) *The Learning Organization*, Fontana, London

Goyder, M. (1994) Foreword to Clarke, T, and Monkhouse, E. (Eds) (1994)

Greiner, L. E. (1972) 'Evolution and Revolution as Organizations Grow', *Harvard Business Review*, 50 (4), pp. 37–46

Hampden-Turner, C. (1992) *Charting the Corporate Mind*, Blackwell, Oxford

Harrison, R. (Fall 1983) 'Strategies for a New Age', *Human Resource Management*, 22 (3), pp. 209–235

Jaques, E. (1970) 'Death and the Mid-life Crisis', in *Work, Creativity and Social Justice*, Heinemann, London

Kimberly, J. R. and Miles, R. H. (1980) *The Organizational Life Cycle*, Jossey Bass, San Francisco

Kouzes, J. M. and Posner, B. Z. (1987) *The Leadership Challenge: How to get extraordinary things done in organizations*, Jossey Bass, San Francisco

Lloyd, T. (1990) *The 'Nice' Company*, Bloomsbury, London

Lievegoed, B. C. G. (1973) *The Developing Organization*, Celestial Arts, Millbrae, California

Morgan, G. (1986) *Images of Organization*, Sage, London

National Small Firms Policy and Research Conference (23 November 1993) *The Guardian*

Pascale, R. (1991) *Managing on the Edge*, Penguin, Harmondsworth, Middlesex

Pedler, M. J., Burgoyne, J. G. and Boydell, T. H. (1991) *The Learning Company: A strategy for sustainable development*, McGraw-Hill, Maidenhead

Porter, M. E. (1980) *Competitive Strategy*, Free Press, New York

Salama, A. (1992) 'The Use of an Organization's Biography as a Research Method for Investigating Organization Development', *Management Education and Development*, 23 (3), pp. 225–33

5   Can big companies really learn?

A survey of large UK organizations came up with the following reasons for the need to learn faster than the rate of change:

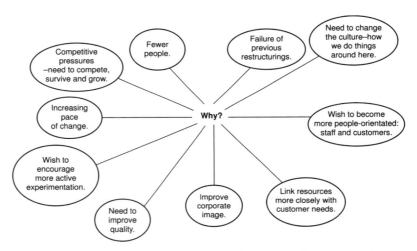

Figure 5.1   Pressures for change and development in large companies
(*Source:* Pedler, Burgoyne and Boydell 1988)

Today, even big companies are seriously concerned about their survival and prosperity. For example, a recent analysis of *Fortune 500* companies showed that the average life expectancy of the US corporation is 45 years and falling (Garratt, 1994, p. 5).

Findings like these concentrate the mind and place a premium on learning. The rational processes of strategic planning have failed these companies, yet wise leadership and direction are crucial as never before. Companies need both to be more cost-conscious *and* more creative; to improve quality to compete and link resources more closely to customer/user needs. Following the ineffectiveness of so much tinkering with structures, there has been great stress on 'changing the culture', a much more difficult undertaking. All this is being done with fewer people as big companies continue to cut staff. This creates pressures on these chosen few in whom there is a correspondingly greater investment and expectations about performance and contribution.

Big is best?

In terms of organizational learning, the main problem big companies have is the downside of their great advantage— size. Companies grow—through horizontal and vertical integration, through acquisition and merger—to try and dominate the markets they serve. Big has proved best in obtaining economies of scale, but it also means big infrastructures, legions of support staff, complex technical and social systems of communication, meetings, relationships.

And another thing; we value large organizations for the services they provide, but do we really like working in them? Big organizations provide income, security, training, a structure for life, all highly desirable things—especially if you don't have them. But, once you do have them, these tend, as Herzberg said, to be 'hygiene' factors that don't motivate. Big companies often find it hard to house highly-motivated, creative, entrepreneurial people.

There is a long history of big organizations trying to stay healthy. In the 1960s and 1970s, organization development (OD) aimed to loosen up the big bureaucracies. Through personal development, teamwork, intergroup conflict resolution and a whole systems perspective, OD promised more fluidity in the rigid, highly differentiated organization where all know their place but not much else. The age of Excellence succeeded OD by the 1980s. For Tom Peters, hankering back to basics and an earlier golden age of small companies and extraordinary service, this robust force did not tinker with bureaucracy but scrapped it. 'Excellence' struck a resounding chord encouraging much 'bureaucracy busting', 'delayering' and 'inverting the pyramid'; it highlighted the importance of 'vision' and 'mission' and empowered front-line workers to make the customer king again.

Excellence is great, but can you keep it up? The evidence from some industries suggests that this is the problem— become excellent, become market leader and, in five or seven years' time, you may well be on the slide. For big companies, the learning company idea is attractive because it might offer a way of staying excellent.

For big companies, the learning company implies that:

- *all staff see themselves as learners on behalf of the company* To keep up with the pace of change people take responsibility for their own personal learning and development. More than this, people need to take responsibility for keeping the company up to date. To achieve this, the way people are managed needs to foster ...
- *self-direction and self-management* Fewer people, more focussed on users and customers means less 'boss-subordinate' management and more self-management. People are proactive and take initiatives rather than being directed and controlled. The company becomes fit ...
- *to house the spirit of self-development* People taking responsibility for their own work/learning need the space and headroom to develop. As responsible adults, peers not subordinates, staff need 'voice' in the organization, an opportunity to have their say and to influence decisions. In a way, the company works ...
- *as a consortium of small businesses* Everyone sees their job as their own business, with all the vitality, energy and effort that this implies. The organization is a collective market with an overarching strategic framework in which people exchange and trade with users, customers and suppliers. The success of this enterprise is everybody's business.

These require health and vitality throughout the company to encourage learning and its application to the work. Check on your company now—how healthy is it?

Application 8: The company health check

1. Thinking of your company, and ignoring for the moment its *financial* health, which of the following would you say best characterized its physical, psychological and cultural condition?

Brilliant, outstanding	☐
Robust	☐
Fair to average	☐
Better than expected, given its age	☐
Improving	☐
Convalescent	☐

Declining ☐

Infirm ☐

Poorly ☐

Paralysed ☐

2. What would you say was the main cause of this condition?

_____

3. What of the future? Will things get better or worse?

_____

It takes sustained effort to stay healthy and 'learningful' in the big, established company. Staying excellent is a condition of survival in highly competitive markets. How do high-profile companies with valuable household name brands keep up? Let's take a look at how SmithKline Beecham is preparing for the future.

CASE: Learning capabilities at SmithKline Beecham

Note: This case is based on work carried out by Terry Hutton and Mike Pedler (UK) with Breck Arnzen and Rick Lent (USA). I am indebted to my colleagues for their contributions, especially Rick for his diagrams. MJP

SmithKline Beecham (SB) was created in 1989 as the result of a merger between the British Beechams and the USA's SmithKline French. SB is one of the biggest pharmaceutical companies in the world employing over 50 000 employees in 120 countries. Apart from pharmaceuticals, SB markets consumer healthcare products such as Lucozade, Ribena, Horlicks, and in the USA, clinical laboratories offering testing services to health services.

This 'true merger of equals' was created deliberately over an extended period. Founded on the relationship between two men, Bob Bauman of Beecham and Henry Wendt of SmithKline Beckman, who met several times early in the process and discovered that 'they saw things in very much the same way'. Even when the merger was declared a year later in July 1989, there were no detailed integration plans. These would involve all SB employees, would be produced over the next six months and implemented over the next year. So the new company, with an unusually well-managed birth, was relatively free from the normal traumas of takeover and had a healthy base from which to develop.

SB's strategy is to move from its old identity as a 'pill manufac-turer' to a company offering integrated healthcare services. To help with this a senior management team began the development of *Simply Better*—a set of guiding values, nine leadership practices and 'The Promise of SmithKline Beecham' to become a *'Simply Better* healthcare company, as judged by all those we serve: customers, shareholders, employees and the global community'. The *Simply Better Way* is a 10:3:1 strategy to bring about the Promise: a 10 year Strategic Intent 'to be the world's best healthcare company'; 3 Year requirements—objectives for specific change areas; and 1 year goals—action steps to fulfil the requirements throughout the company at all business unit levels.

The R & D Division is at the core of SB's business, providing the basis for future products in the highly competitive global health-care market. The Human Resource Development Managers, Breck Arnzen, based in the USA, and Terry Hutton, based in the UK, are the leaders of a project to develop a worldwide training needs analysis process for the R & D business. The purpose of this process is to ensure that the people in SB have the skills and capabilities to meet the future business challenges. Given the rapid rate of change, how can this be done? And, in this era of the Learning Company, how valid is the notion of a 'Training Needs Analysis' anyway?

The future business—some predictions
In common with the rest of the industry, SB is meeting tougher conditions in its markets. In the face of increased pressures on prices by governments in Europe, the USA and elsewhere, SB will be forced to reduce its fixed costs and is likely to employ fewer people. This will mean changed working practices, a flattening of the organization, an increase in contracting out and generally more flexibility of organization and people.

These likely changes point to various requirements for the capabilities, competencies and skills of people. Good project man-agement will be ever more vital in the race to reduce development cycle times of clinical projects. Interpersonal skills of the lateral, supply chain sort will be crucial. People will be more self-reliant self-starters and, at the same time, many of those with little previous experience of exercising power and authority will have it thrust upon them. Teamworking will need to be multi-disciplinary, not just within a single discipline. Managers will be 'clucking hens rather than strutting cockerels'—mothering their project teams, offering advice and chasing results, rather than bossing and controlling them.

Three approaches to future skills analysis in SB   Training Needs Analysis (TNA) is the traditional way of identifying the skills and knowledge requirements for companies. However, in these fast-moving times, there are limitations to the traditional methods. What sort of methods are appropriate?

Three approaches have emerged chronologically which are all still potentially relevant. Early examples of TNA go back to 1940s Armed Forces' practices. By the 1960s and '70s TNA practices had developed widely in the UK and USA in an era of 'systematic training'. This approach, based on identifying the gap between the skills and knowledge of particular individuals and the requirements of particular jobs, gives us a first clear focus:

1. Individual Capability *This approach sets out to specify the skill, knowledge or attitude requirements of an individual (or group of similar individuals) in relation to a specific job or position. Training can be prescribed to fill the gap between individual capabilities and job requirements. The term 'individual capability' as opposed to 'individual need' stresses effective actions ie outputs rather than inputs—of skill, knowledge, attitude and so on. Traditionally this method tends to operate in the here and now—on the current job—but increasingly future capabilities are considered.*

A second focus has emerged more recently and reflects the increased importance of team performance in organizations:

2. Workplace Capability *puts the emphasis upon defining the capabilities required to perform a job, function or process, rather than on the individual. Training can help develop capability through learning events which provide experience and feedback. Here competent performance depends more on the capabilities of the team, group or supply chain and less upon the capabilities of any one individual.*

The latest way in which we can frame TNA is in the context of the Learning Company with a view to promoting organizational learning:

3. Organizational Capability *concerned with developing the ability or capacity to work, learn and enquire together as a whole company. This involves the creation, collection, diffusion and use of new knowledge and know-how as well as maintaining and developing the core competencies which differentiate the enterprise. Training sets out to facilitate the growth and sharing of knowledge across the organization and with the surrounding environment.*

The main points of the three approaches, together with some key questions and methods which might apply in that approach, are:

Table 5.1   Three approaches to TNA

Approach	Key questions	Methods
Individual capability	Who needs to know what? What capabilities does this person need to succeed in their current job? What future capabilities might be required in these jobs? What capabilities does this person need for their future career?	Appraisal and performance reviews Career planning and personal development plans
Workplace capability	What constitutes good performance in this job or function or process? What capabilities are required to perform well as a team, group or supply chain? What future capabilities will be needed?	Competency modelling Benchmarking Prototyping Cherrypicking Team/process analysis
Organizational capability	What are the core competencies of the company and on what capabilities are these based? Does the organization have the ability to learn, grow and change appropriately? Does the company have the ability to create and disseminate new knowledge? Does the organization have the capability needs to fulfil its vision?	Core competencies Strategic planning Scenario planning Learning company Measure rate of organizational learning—'knowledge turns'

Combined tactics?   The best way ahead for SB rests in using a combination of these three approaches. In terms of *Individual Capability*, the job can safely be left with managers and team leaders with the tools and processes already at their disposal. In SB, these individual-level processes for identifying and meeting learning needs are well understood and practised.

In terms of *Organizational Capability*, SB has more work to do to create a vision for assessment and development that will fit *Simply Better* and the *Simply Better Way*. However, it is clear that the approach must change the thinking about Training Needs Analysis:

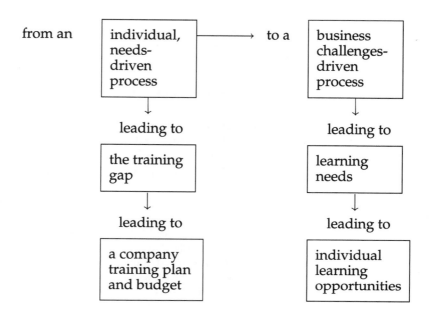

This second way of thinking is the one which can contribute best towards SB's 10:3:1 strategy and ensure that the challenges facing the Company generate the learning responses rather than the training programmes determining the skills and capabilities that people have (and don't have).

In terms of the middle category of *Workplace Capability*, one exciting idea is to create a venture fund to which departments, process teams, functions or units make bids for their own ideas for training and development projects. Open competition for the available funds puts the Human Resources Development function in 'Venture Capitalist' mode, determining the criteria for selection and requiring evaluation and reporting of the added value from successful projects. As with *Organizational Capability*, this should ensure that training and development programmes are business needs-driven, but there will be an element of risk—that of the HRD manager sticking his neck out and committing the funds to the likely future 'winners'. This will take courage in giving up the old, comfortable pattern of spending the budget on an extensive programme of courses.

Can big companies really learn?

The SB case gives us a glimpse of how one big company is working to stay in shape and prepare itself for future challenges. However, it would be unwise to assume that learning just naturally follows from the identification of desired individual, workplace and organizational capabilities.

As we've seen, even small companies tend to lose the 'natural' ability to learn at a comparatively early age and must take special steps to rediscover the learning habit. These are companies small enough for one person or a small group to make that happen. This is much more complicated in the big company. Can they really revitalize and reinvent themselves or is this so much PR?

As the turbulence in the environment increases and the lifecycle of the company shortens, we are likely to see more stories like that about Wang Laboratories.

> In August 1992, Wang Laboratories, once a $3 billion powerhouse of the computing industry, filed for bankruptcy protection after losses of over $1.5 billion in four years—a victim of the recession, failing to adapt to rapid technological change. The company is planning to shed 5000 of their remaining 13 000 staff—down from the late 1980s peak of 31 500 people.
>
> Founded in 1951 by a Chinese immigrant An Wang, the company pioneered word processing equipment and flourished in the 1970s and early 1980s. However Wang was focused on mid-sized computers using proprietary systems and was slow to adapt to the advent of personal computers. Poor management by Mr Wang's son and heir Frederick accelerated the decline. A new Chairman was brought in at a salary of $1 million in 1989 and promised a 'new Wang', but, having been previously with General Electric's TV operations, he had no experience of the computer world, and the turnaround did not happen.
>
> (Source: M. Tran 1992.)

The Wang story reminds us that, in computing, failure is part of the game. The events at Wang are overshadowed by the struggles of the giant IBM, whose founder once declaimed 'Learning is our business—we just sell the by-products of that learning'. For connoisseurs of self-sabotaging prophecies, this is a good one. A recent newspaper report reveals that the new boss of IBM has gone through the old strategic plans back to 1980 and discovered that the company foresaw the shift away from mainframes as far back as that. Unfortunately, it was unable to act at that time. The head thinks, but the legs won't move.

In the fast-paced computer business, the real test of a company's mettle is not whether it slips or not, but if it can learn from the inevitable mistakes and recover quickly. If you get thrown off the merry-go-round at one side you have to bounce back and get on at the other. Wang has now recovered to remain something of a player in this business game, and IBM is trying to revitalize. Trying to get it 'right first time' misses the point; a healthy response encourages experiment, expects mistakes and is quick to *act*.

Another aspect of the Wang story illustrates how some big commercial companies are just like their smaller cousins, especially where ownership remains tightly controlled by a few people. A colleague researched the private-sector steel industry of Sheffield in the 1950s and found a long tradition of father-son succession. She delighted in telling of the folk wisdom she uncovered there: that, for owners, it was a good thing when the owner was blessed with daughters rather than with sons, for the daughters could be encouraged to marry the best young prospects in the firm.

So, what stops us learning?

We have taken children, with their normally rapid and joyful progress, as our models for learning theories, and assumed that to learn is natural and easy. In fact, as Roger Harrison has reminded us, as adults we struggle between an urge to defend our adult selves and a need to know new things—'to a large extent, we *are* our defences'. Argyris has made a similar point about organizational 'defensive routines' that make uncomfortable things undiscussable. Yet, as Pascale has pointed out, some conflict is necessary for learning; without the ability to disagree, we suppress or deny knowledge and information for fear of rocking the boat.

However, sometimes the reason we fail to learn is much simpler than this. In big companies, in particular, so much knowledge and information is not collected or passed on and is simply forgotten. To re-quote Argyris and Schon:

> There are too many cases in which organizations know less than their members. There are even cases in which the organization cannot seem to learn what every member knows.
>
> (1978, p. 9)

Or, as someone put it, 'If only we knew what we know'! In setting out on the road to becoming a learning company, the first step is to assess how the company learns at present. The second is to ask, 'How could we improve on this?' One company instituted a 'time in job' project because it was concerned about the loss of 'systemic wisdom'. The symptoms were:

- a rapid turnover of people posts, especially, but not only, in the marketing operation
- complaints and demotivation from 'high flyers' and 'fast movers' if they were stuck in a post for more than two years

- a lack of stability in key functions due to loss of knowledge—one director of an important subsidiary found himself, after one year's service, to be the longest-serving Board member
- an increase in the use of outside consultants to buy the 'old wisdom'.

Losing your memory?

This is the most fundamental challenge to companies wishing to improve their organizational learning: the first thing to do is to make sure you're making the best of what is available.

The simplest level of learning is memory. Can we remember what we've learned? The recipe for a particular product? How to handle the quirks of a long-standing customer? Loss of organizational memory can be a serious problem for companies, particularly in fast-changing times with a rapid turnover of key people.

> Few companies have problems as serious as the US Department of Energy's concerns about the 27 tons of plutonium that it has stored in sites around the USA. A few grains of plutonium is enough to kill you; 10 kilograms will make a large bomb and, in 24 000 years, half of this 27 tons will still be active. On top of this, many of the storage sites are not very safe. Threatened by earthquake fears in California, by obsolete or bulging containers elsewhere and generally by badly maintained safety systems, 300 'vulnerables' have been identified on 13 sites.
>
> It emerges that there has been an alarming loss of 'institutional memory' and expertise at many sites as senior engineers retire or leave. At the Savannah River plant in South Carolina, plutonium production ceased in 1988 and now more than 60 per cent of the engineers on staff have never seen the plant operate.
>
> (*The Guardian*, 1st September, 1994)

Loss of organizational memory affects all companies, but it is an especial problem for big ones, because they have so much of it stored in departmental records and individual human minds all over the place. In a small company, you can usually find your way around this crucial database by asking, but how do you do this in a multinational, grown huge in the quick and modern way of acquisition and merger?

Here is an example of a big company tackling this problem and going about the process of making sure it knows all its people know about important aspects of the business.

CASE: United Distillers and worldwide learning

United Distillers (UD) is a multinational drinks company operating with famous brands—including Johnnie Walker Scotch Whisky and Gordon's Gin—around the world. UD is, in some ways, a young organization, born only in 1987 as a result of the Guinness acquisition of the Distillers Company Limited and Arthur Bell Distillers. On the other hand, it has a long tradition in the 'heritage' business of Scottish whisky making.

Transnational business

Today, UD seeks competitive advantage by operating in a world-wide market. Between 1989 and 1992, the acquisition of distribution around the world gave significant but one-off profit growth. Now, as the industry consolidates around four big international spirits companies, together with a myriad of local manufacturers, competition in the world spirits market is intense, and global brands are the key to success.

It is important for UD to learn about how to build brands around the world and to deliver customer service. Transfer of learning and experience throughout the company is a crucial aspect of organizational effectiveness when competing either in the mature, flat markets of Europe and the USA or in building brands in the emerging markets of Asia, Eastern Europe or Latin America. As competitors have access to similar technologies, sources of capital, skills and expertise, there is a premium on management and organizational effectiveness—especially, perhaps, organizational learning processes:

> In such international industries as we define them, the key to success lay in the ability to transfer knowledge to overseas units and to manage the product lifecycle efficiently and flexibly ... This ability to learn and to appropriate the benefits of learning in multiple national markets differentiated the winners from the losers in this highly complex business.
>
> (Bartlett and Ghoshal, 1989, pp. 24 and 25)

Bartlett and Ghoshal suggest three necessary capabilities for successful 'transnational management'—global integration, national responsiveness and worldwide learning. To manage worldwide learning, companies have to simultaneously encourage local innovations and implement the best of them on a global basis. This is tricky because:

> ... independent and resource-rich subsidiaries tend to become victims of what Rosabeth Kantor calls the 'entrepreneurial trap'—a mentality in which 'the need to be the source, the originator leads people to push their own ideas single-mindedly'. As companies like Philips have found, this mentality impedes the subsidiary's ability and willingness to adopt central innovations.
>
> (Bartlett and Ghoshal, 1989, p. 123)

In other words, the more innovative we are, the more we tend to reject others' ideas on the 'not invented here' basis. Is this true or can companies that develop good organizational learning capabilities both invent *and* adopt?

Less global integration, more worldwide learning
In 1989, UD was focusing hard on achieving global integration of its worldwide businesses. This entailed the establishment of a company style—'The UD Way'—and its inculcation in all parts of the business. By 1994, Human Resources Director Mike Pemberton's view is that they have moved from a two-dimensional world of balancing integration and market responsiveness to a three-dimensional world where global integration and market responsiveness are balanced with the need to effectively transfer best practice and learning from one part of the company to another—shared worldwide learning, as shown in Figure 5.2.

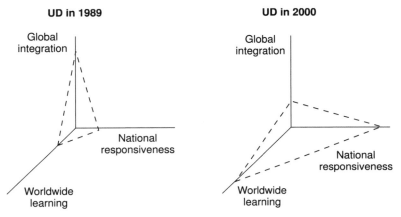

Figure 5.2　UD and Worldwide Learning

An increasingly important part of UD's strategy concerns joint ventures (JVs). JVs offered a quick way to build distribution around the world in the late 1980s, whereas the ownership of a 34 per cent stake in Moet Hennessy represents a much longer term strategic alliance. Approximately 40 per cent of UD's profits already come from JVs—a proportion that may well increase—and this means that added value comes from UD's ability to improve management processes in organizations owned by *other* companies as well as in its own, wholly owned subsidiaries.

Key learning groups　Key learning groups (KLGs) are Mike Pemberton's idea for bringing about more worldwide learning. KLGs are designed to bring about organizational learning through the systematic retrieval, storage and transmission of know-how about particular aspects of the business. KLGs aim to create a space in the fast-paced life of the business in which people can reflect on learning and have the opportunity to transfer it—making learning a conscious organizational endeavour.

The first three KLGs in UD deal with acquisitions, joint ventures and major restructurings. These are all critical aspects of managing this global company and matters in which UD has considerable experience held in various companies and individuals. Although people make presentations at conferences to share their experiences, without a systematic process, this learning can be lost or overlooked, with the result that parts of the business may repeat, unknowingly, mistakes made elsewhere. The aim of the KLGs is to make local knowledge available companywide.

This last point is particularly important because of the third 'arm' of Bartlett and Ghoshal's model. Big multi- or transnationals like UD cannot impose a corporate will on their empires in the way some of them did formerly, because country companies must be free to operate as only they know how in their local markets. UD's British senior managers are perhaps not best placed for making all the decisions about selling French brandy in China or South American rum in the Phillipines. This requirement for 'local responsiveness' means that country companies are likely to do some things differently and create the variety of processes that is the seedcorn for worldwide learning.

Each KLG has a Sponsors Group of key informants who design the initial model, own the process and sign off the output. A Review Group of executives from various countries tests, challenges and enriches the model. This group includes people likely to be involved in disseminating the output. The process followed by each KLG involves:

- collecting experience and learning from people, and data from various 'archives'
- clarifying and summarizing the learning to establish 'best demon-strated practice'
- disseminating the learning throughout the organization to appro-priate audiences, via appropriate media.

While the product of a KLG makes a valuable contribution, KLGs are also in themselves organizational learning *processes*. Such processes contribute in a wider way by stimulating and supporting continuing learning worldwide on important business issues, partly through raising the level of skills and resources to make this more likely and partly through improving the worldwide learning climate.

Integrating the big company through organizational learning processes

Integration is always needed in companies, but takes different forms. In the small company, the integrating force may be the personality or beliefs of the founder; in the administrative organization, the system of rules and procedures. As a big company, we might expect UD to have developed all manner of bureaucratic devices to integrate its widespread operations. In fact, the company was born big and is described by one manager as:

> ... a toddler, with no maturity of the management processes you would expect in a company of this size. We didn't grow naturally ... but were born as a large monolith and had to learn how to operate from there.

Again, all companies are unique, however they may conform in terms of their outside appearances, public images and so on. UD's biography means that even experienced people need to learn to manage in *this* company. Past history demonstrates that even highly rated executives who come in from other companies, even multinational, 'fast-moving consumer goods' organizations, can misunderstand how UD works. One such experience was summed up as follows:

> They thought that if you pulled a lever at the top, a whole machinery would click smoothly into place all the way down ... in UD, if you pull such a lever it is likely to come off in your hand!

An age that has learned about the downside of bureaucracy as an approach to integration has also invented organizational learning as an alternative. Learning through sharing—where people in parts of the company are teachers *and* learners together—can provide a new form of integration, creating connectedness and a sense of community.

In an informal culture like UD's, it is an important part of many managers' jobs to put people in touch with one another to share their experience of what they're doing, what has worked and what hasn't. KLGs and other organizational learning processes are trying to encourage this sort of learning habit on a more widespread basis.

The way in which such processes are developed is crucial; cloning or imposing accumulated wisdom will not do. In matters of organizational memory, the obvious trap is in creating an over-respect for the past that works against future creativity. The KLG process must somehow be an ongoing one, encouraging continuous learning as well as capturing and disseminating the fruits of past experience.

Organizational learning styles

Tapping the experience and knowledge of all the people who work in the business and improving organizational memory is a good place to start in establishing the learning company. However, this is just a start. There are many other opportunities to learn, and the healthy company will not rely on just one style or method of learning.

The dangers of relying on just one method of learning are twofold. First, we might miss out on ideas and innovations that come via other routes. Second, the overuse of any one particular way of learning can actually cause damage. Take organizational memory—the retrieval and storage of past experience and knowledge—as an example. Clearly, superb information systems and accessible databases will be an asset to any business, especially in empowering people to act quickly on the company's behalf. However, if we just rely on this way of learning and working, then we might create too much reliance on solutions that worked in the past or encourage people to look up the answers instead of experimenting and investigating elsewhere.

The questionnaire that follows is based on a model of organizational learning modes or styles developed in writing this book. As is usual with such things, it owes much to other people's ideas, especially to Roger Stuart's notion of 'paradigms' for the learning organization .

Using the questionnaire, you can test out the way, or ways, in which your company as a whole tends to learn, and also spot which ways of learning are underused. Fill out the questionnaire first, then score it and the results will be explained once you have a profile for your company

Big companies do it through partnerships

In this chapter we've discussed some of the problems of bigness when it comes to learning and looked at some of the ways in which big companies are trying to keep themselves fit, healthy and continuing to learn. Big commercial companies, exposed to hypercompetitive global markets, are more and more aware of how difficult it is to stay with, let alone ahead of, the game. They are aware that being big and successful can contain the seeds of its own destruction. This is perhaps the single most powerful reason for the current popularity of ideas about organizational learning.

So far in this chapter we've talked about what a company can do to help itself. Another very important aspect of the learning company is what we have termed 'intercompany learning' (Pedler, Burgoyne and Boydell, 1991, p. 22). This aspect is only touched on in the organizational learning styles inventory under the 'imitating' mode, which is a rather limited way of thinking about the possibilities of learning from other companies. We can use the learning company idea to reframe the variety of business partnerships in which big companies are increasingly engaged. For example, the United Distillers case earlier touches on joint ventures and partnerships as a vital avenue of learning for big companies.

Various forms of strategic alliance have become an integral part of contemporary strategic thinking. The takeover boom

Application 9: Organizational learning styles inventory

This questionnaire takes the form of seven incomplete sentences, each of which has five possible completing statements.

For each of the incomplete sentences, you have 12 points to allocate among the 5 statements accompanying it, depending on how typical of your company you think it is. For example, if you think that 1 of the 5 *absolutely* describes your company, while none of the other 4 does at all, then you could give 12 points to that 1 statement. More likely, you will want to distribute your 12 points among the 5, giving most points to that which best describes your company and few or no points to that which least describes your company. The more you are able to discriminate, the clearer will be the organizational learning style of your company.

A In this company, we are really good at . . .

1. operating to standard procedures ☐
2. collecting and storing knowledge and data ☐
3. benchmarking best practice from other companies ☐
4. innovating and finding new ways of doing things ☐
5. being critically aware of what is going on in our world ☐

Total points   12

B The most respected people in this company are those who . . .

1. do things according to the book ☐
2. know a great deal about our business ☐
3. bring in lots of new ideas from other companies ☐
4. develop new ideas and practices on the job ☐
5. are always asking questions about the way we do things ☐

Total points   12

C What we're most likely to say about ourselves is that we have . . .

1. first-class operating systems ☐
2. databases and information back-up unmatched in our field ☐
3. excellent networking with other organizations ☐
4. an experimental, 'leading edge' reputation ☐
5. wide vision and take a long view ☐

Total points   12

D What we're least likely to say is ...

1. 'No one sings from the same hymn sheet' ☐

2. 'history is bunk' ☐

3. 'we've got nothing to learn from the opposition' ☐

4. 'if it ain't broke, don't fix it' ☐

5. 'go for the quick fix every time' ☐

Total points 12

E When there's a crisis, we ...

1. remain calm and continue with the correct procedure ☐

2. search for data and precedents we can learn from ☐

3. ring round our contacts and ask their advice ☐

4. drop everything else and get stuck in—we love it! ☐

5. act only after mature consideration of the wider implications

   of possible actions ☐

Total points 12

F Our biggest weakness is ...

1. getting stuck in fixed ways of responding ☐

2. depending on things that worked well for us in the past ☐

3. relying too much on other people's ideas ☐

4. reinventing everything—even when they work OK ☐

5. losing clear, short-term focus ☐

Total points 12

G The most pressing priority for change in this company is to ...

1. loosen up and give people more discretion and responsibility ☐

2. develop a future orientation and vision ☐

3. encourage people inside to develop their own ideas ☐

4. strengthen operating procedures and cut down on experiment

   for experiment's sake ☐

5. balance short- and long-term foci ☐

Total points 12

Scoring

Transfer your total points for each sentence to the table.

	1	2	3	4	5
A					
B					
C					
D					
E					
F					
G					
Totals					

The higher your score for 1, 2, 3, 4 or 5, the *more* your company tends to use this style of learning according to your responses.

The lower your score for 1, 2, 3, 4 or 5, the *less* your company tends to use this style of learning according to your responses.

The numbers 1, 2, 3, 4 and 5 correspond to the following organizational learning styles:
1 = habits
2 = memory
3 = imitation
4 = experiment
5 = awareness.

Figure 5.3 outlines the characteristics of each of these styles.

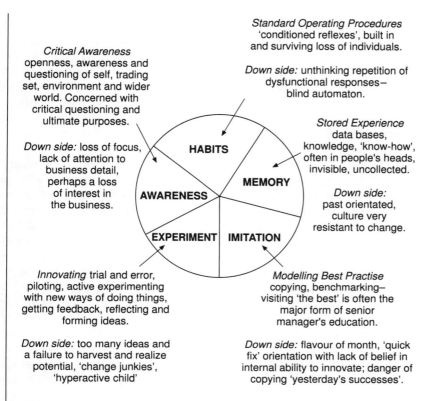

Figure 5.3   Organizational learning styles inventory

How does your company shape up in terms of its learning styles?

A large score for one of the five modes or styles suggests a company preference for that way of doing things, while a low score indicates that this way of learning is underused. A fairly equal distribution of points could suggest that the company is balanced and multiskilled at learning; on the other hand, it might mean that it doesn't really have any learning strengths at all—it's just that you had to allocate the points somewhere!

What this means is that you have to use the questionnaire in a thoughtful way—perhaps to check against other evidence or as the basis for a discussion among a group of people concerned with this aspect of company performance. As with all other such devices, you put the data in and it's up to you to do what you want with what comes out—if it's not useful to you, junk it and try something else.

We should say here that this questionnaire has not yet been rigorously validated, but that early experiments are promising, showing that people can use the model to discriminate and that scores have some considerable face validity in terms of people's experiences of their companies' learning cultures.

of the acquisitive 1980s has given way to the notion of partnership, and there is a rising wave of cooperative agreements described by some as the 'competitive weapon of the 1990s'. In the face of rising competition, disillusioned with acquisitions that fail to live up to their apparent promise and fuelled by TQM notions, such as 'preferred supplier', many companies, even competitors, are looking to share costs and resources to create new products, acquire new technology, enter new markets.

However, partnerships are notoriously difficult. One study reports that less than a third of strategic alliances meet or exceed expectations; and another that about a third were failures. Failure rates as high as 70 per cent within 3 years for joint ventures is reported in one study, and another notes that 75 per cent end in acquisitions by one party. Transnational partnerships seem to have an even slimmer chance of success—meshing corporate cultures and styles is tough enough for partners who speak the same language and who know each other's operations. Companies are criticized for being naïve and urged to plan for the worst. The costs of divorce include stress, anxiety and conflict within the company.

This suggests that takeover or acquisition is still more palatable or easier to manage for most companies (although the evidence for the success of takeovers is hardly better), yet, despite the pitfalls, most commentators remain bullish about the value of partnering.

For Kanter, 'collaborative advantage' is now a key corporate asset that stems from the ability to be a good partner. Good partners can create alliances that are living systems, evolving progressively to enable partners to create new value together rather than just doing deals based on quick returns on investment. Such partnerships cannot be controlled by formal systems, but require:

> a dense web of interpersonal connections and internal infrastructures that enhance learning.
>
> (Kanter, 1994)

Partnerships that are based on long-term commitment rather than a basis for short-term financial gains could overcome some of the learning difficulties faced by big companies. The lack of conflict and the tendency to conform in many large organizations has been identified by Pascale as a major barrier to creating a learning organization. Partnerships of different but equal parties with dense webs of interpersonal connections and internal infrastructures are unlikely to have this problem.

The very problems inherent in joint ventures and other strategic alliances are, therefore, potentially great learning opportunities for the partners. One commentator notes that:

> How well a firm benefits depends on how it works on the inside. The need for close cooperation with others imposes a distinct set of requirements on the firm. Amongst these are the need for substantial delegation and an unprecedented emphasis on organizational learning.
>
> (Lewis, 1991)

Another, that alliances should be structured as:

> ... learning platforms to assimilate new technologies and skills to revitalize their core operations and find new uses for existing skills.
>
> (Lei, 1993)

Partnerships are an avenue for learning that is currently underused by many big companies. The emphasis on competition and 'competitive advantage' has encouraged a self-sufficiency and an isolationism that militates against shared learning with other companies. If Kanter and others are right, then these attitudes need to be unlearned quickly so that the skills of cooperation and intercompany connection can be developed.

If partnerships and intercompany learning are an opportunity for big commercial companies, they amount to an urgent necessity in public service—the focus of the next chapter. The demands now being made on our schools, hospitals, police forces, social services, housing agencies and so on can only be met through increasing interagency cooperation. Chapter 6 looks at this and other related questions in the public services to see how organizational learning and the learning company can help with these fundamentals of our society. As with the other specific locations for organizational learning theory and practice in this book, the public services are particularly well-placed for illuminating certain aspects of managing and organizing because some of the problems they face are peculiar to them. However, the lessons learned—for example, about joint development work with other agencies or managing professionals—have a wider relevance.

References

Argyris, C. and Schon, D. (1978) *Organizational Learning: A Theory of Action Perspective*, Addison-Wesley, Reading, Massachusetts

Bartlett, C. A. and Ghoshal, S. (1989) *Managing Across Borders: The transnational solution*, Hutchinson, London

Garratt, R. (Ed.) (1994) *Developing Strategic Thinking*, McGraw-Hill, Maidenhead

Harrison, R. (1995) 'Defences and the Need to Know', in Harrison, R. *Collected Works*, McGraw-Hill, Maidenhead

Kanter, R. M. (July/August 1994) 'Collaborative Advantage: The Art of Alliances', *Harvard Business Review*

Lei, D. (1993) 'Offensive and Defensive Uses of Alliances', *Long Range Planning*, 26 (4)

Lewis, J. D. (April 1991) 'Competitive Alliances Re-define Companies', *Management Review*, 80 (4)

Pascale, R. T. (1991) *Managing on the Edge*, Penguin, Harmondsworth, Middlesex

Pedler, M. J., Burgoyne, J. G. and Boydell, T. H. (1988) *The Learning Company Project Report*, Training Agency, Sheffield

Pedler, M. J., Burgoyne, J. G. and Boydell, T. H. (1991) *The Learning Company: A strategy for sustainable development*, McGraw-Hill, Maidenhead

Stuart, R. and Norton, A. 'Paradigms for Learning Organization', in Boydell, T. *et al.* (1994) *Learning Company Conference Papers 1994*, Learning Company Project, Sheffield

Tran, M. (18 and 19 August 1992) articles in *The Guardian*

6   Learning for public service

Learning to manage ambiguity and paradox is a recurring theme in this book, and nowhere is there more experience of balancing diverse interests and meeting multiplying and sometimes contradictory demands than in the public sector. Yet, this sector is rarely seen by itself or by others as a rich source of organizational learning. This chapter will attempt to change this view by highlighting lessons from public sector experience that are of wider application.

Perhaps the most fundamental paradox or key dilemma for a public service is that, identified by Michael Barber from Keele University, of providing for both *equality* and *diversity*. He uses the well-known terms from *1066 and All That* to typify the alternatives, shown in Figure 6.1.

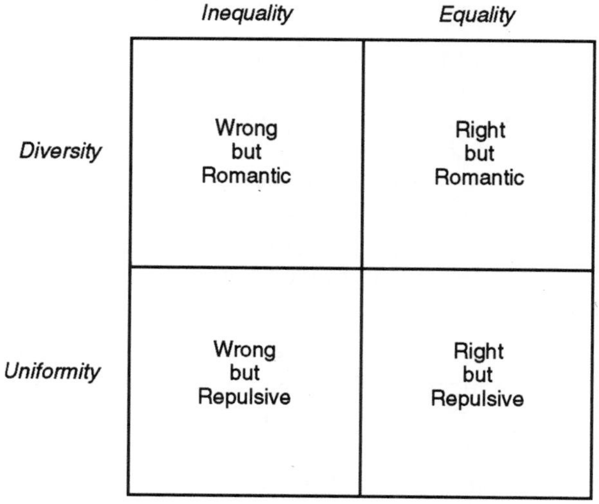

	Inequality	Equality
Diversity	Wrong but Romantic	Right but Romantic
Uniformity	Wrong but Repulsive	Right but Repulsive

Figure 6.1   Equality and diversity

In Figure 6.1, uniformity is always seen to be *wrong* and diversity always *romantic*. In the UK, the political parties have tended to occupy either the upper left or lower right quadrants. Barber suggests that the challenge lies in finding the policies and the means that will enable us to combine equality *and* diversity in what is provided from the public purse. However, providing diverse services able to meet differing but equally important needs and choices is not easy. A common error is to benefit some while being unaware or unheedful of the damage to others. Maintaining a balance is inherently unstable and will require constant attention, but is the challenge that faces public service into the next century.

The diversity of the public sector itself makes generalization difficult. What is and what is not part of the public sector varies over time and from country to country. In Italy, for example, banks, airlines, insurance companies and food retailers are all to be found in the public sector, while in the USA healthcare is mainly provided privately. In Britain, some institutions, like The Post Office have (so far) always been publicly owned and run, while others like the railways or the steel industry, have been both public and private at various times. The nature of the public sector is constantly changing; the recent push towards privatization being the latest episode.

In Britain, the sector has traditionally had three discernible areas:

- nationalized industries, many of which have now been reprivatized
- public utilities, most of which have been recently privatized, but where the public interest is intended to be protected by a regulator
- public services—health, education, social services, police, local and central government and so on—which are largely, but by no means entirely, free at the point of delivery.

This chapter will focus on this third part of the public sector, with most of the examples being taken from health and education. It opens with an exploration of the concept of public service itself. What does this mean? How important is it? How is it changing to meet future needs?

We then draw out two main sources of organizational experience and learning that demand to be shared more widely. The first of these is that of learning from and for public accountability. Public servants have a long history of being held to account, dating back at least to Gladstone's

Public Accounts Committee document of 1854. As a consequence of this, accountability has been described as 'extensive' in the public sector and as 'relatively restricted' in the private sector (Harrow and Wilcocks, 1990). As the debate of business ethics grows, experiences of dealing with issues of probity, openness and public accountability become increasingly valuable.

The second, and linked, theme is that of *working with and managing professionals*. Public service professional organizations and unions have, and continue to, resisted elements of the 'reforms' of their services and have been roundly criticized in so doing as acting out of self-interest. While accepting the very real need for change, we explore these issues and look at the more positive side of professionalism, with examples of learning through the voluntary lowering of barriers and the acceptance of new kinds of accountability.

What we mean by public service is partly defined by the very nature of *public accountability*. These services are subject to more than one kind of accountability and as 'there is no unattested goal which provides a criteria for choosing options' (Elcock, 1994, p. 56), there is a need for sensitivity and balance. In this, issues of professionalism and of managing professionals play a key part.

We are not concerned in this chapter with the public sector as such and with what should or should not be part of it. We are concerned with the concept of *public service* and the related notion of the *public good*. As times and services move on, there are things to preserve as well as to change. As we shall see in later chapters, the ethic of public service should not be seen as the exclusive property of the public sector—it is relevant to all parts of the economy.

What is public service?

I've been amazed by the level of commitment I have found amongst the staff. It is the kind of thing the private sector strives for but I have never met anything like it.
(Non-executive member of a NHS Trust board, new to the NHS but with extensive private-sector experience)

People in the health service hold themselves to be much more accountable than anyone I have met in the private sector.
(Management consultant with extensive public- and private-sector experience)

The words *public* and *service* have significant connotations. *The Concise Oxford Dictionary* defines 'service' as the act of serving, helping or benefiting; conduct tending to the welfare or advantage of another. It also offers an interesting set of definitions of 'public':

- 'of or pertaining to the people as a whole'
- 'done or made by or on behalf of the community as a whole'
- 'open to, or shared by members of the community'
- 'open to general observation, existing, done or made in public, manifest not concealed'.

Farnham and Horton identify an impressive list of the characteristics of:

> a public service ethic—equity, fairness, honesty, probity, altruism and trust combined with the ethics of the public service professions to protect 'the public interest'.
>
> (1994, p. 254)

Working to such aspirations demands a great deal. Consider the problems of providing any service that comes up to these standards. In a small town, the parks officer realizes that a few trees in a local park need to be felled because of their age. For this to take place, he has to convince both the local councillors and the community that the trees are becoming dangerous. He has to write a report and take it to the relevant council committee, which meets at six-weekly intervals. As the Council is feeling rather sensitive about this issue after experiencing considerable opposition to a quite different tree-felling request, it asks for further information for the next meeting.

To ensure that the park's users understand the need for felling, the parks officer holds public meetings and talks to local residents who have a particular affection for the park. Not only does the process take time, but the outcome also feels unpredictable. Naturally, if the request is turned down, the officer will not want to be held responsible for any accidents. If the councillors turn it down in direct response to local protest, where will the responsibility lie?

This is one small example of the difficulty of providing a local *public* service. John Stewart summarizes the key tasks facing public services as:

- having political sensitivity, awareness and understanding—managing the political professional divide
- managing public pressure and protest—giving people a voice and managing the consequences
- marketing for equity—establishing, finding and meeting need

- managing the rationing of public services—when demand outstrips supply
- being publicly accountable—and promoting the notion of citizenship
- measuring performance—with a mass of potential competing indicators
- managing strategy—for social change rather than competitive advantage. (1989, pp. 168–75)

These are even more complicated than they look because, in daily practice—as we saw from the parks officer example—they are combined and entwined. Public servants are not infrequently in the position of being publicly accountable for rationed services that aim at equitable treatment, but for which there are no universally agreed performance indicators. Suggestions on a postcard please!

At the same time, other changes are necessary. For example, the demand for responsive local services means that the old professional and organizational 'smokestacks' and boundaries between health, social services, education, police, probation and so on, must yield to collaborative partnerships and cross-agency local planning and action.

Accountability, probity and openness

Being publicly accountable is a key issue for public services and a potentially rich source of learning. For example, the need to be 'manifest, not concealed', in the dictionary definition, is emphasized in The Code of Conduct for NHS Boards, which speaks of 'three crucial public service values' that underpin the work of the NHS. These are:

> *Accountability*—everything done by those who work in the NHS must be able to stand the test of parliamentary scrutiny, public judgements on propriety and professional codes of conduct.
> *Probity*—there should be an absolute standard of honesty in dealing with the assets of the NHS: integrity should be the hallmark of all personal conduct in decisions affecting patients, staff and suppliers, and in the use of information acquired in the course of NHS duties.
> *Openness*—there should be sufficient transparency about NHS activities to promote confidence between the NHS authority or trust and its staff, patients and the public.

> (DoH, 1994, p. 2)

The development of an explicit code of conduct followed

some serious scandals in parts of the service where probity and accountability seemed to have been forgotten in the rush to become entrepreneurial, free from 'red tape'.

There are many people and groups who take a direct interest in whether or not public services are living up to their high aspirations. For example, Pollitt and Harrison pointed out that, in 1991, a District General Manager in the NHS needed to maintain relationships between:

> ... at minimum ... the Regional General Manager, the District Health Authority, the Community Health Council, the managers of local provider units, the local representatives of the British Medical Association, the Royal College of Nursing, the National Union of Public Employees, and the Confederation of Health Service Employees, local councillors and the local MP, the local Social Services Department and the press.
>
> (1991, p. 5).

The Citizens' Charter encourages individuals to add themselves to this list.

Not all those with an interest in a service will agree on what is necessary. One local education authority put on a course designed to support their headteachers. At an early stage in the programme, the heads were asked to draw themselves in their roles. Three images dominated the responses of over 200 headteachers: a juggler, a plate spinner and diagrams like Figure 6.2.

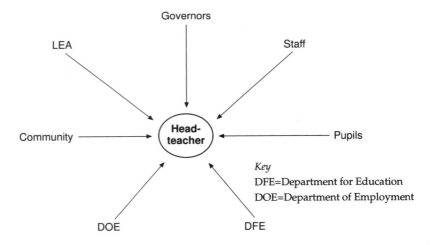

Figure 6.2

The heads saw themselves as needing to respond to the needs or requirements of a variety of individuals and groups. No one saw themselves as propelled along by *shared* demands, as in Figure 6.3.

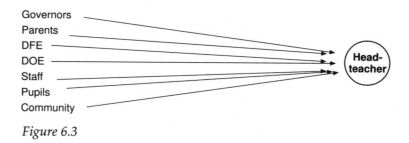

Figure 6.3

All saw the requirements as at best, differing and at worst, contradictory, but that their job required them to learn both how to hold the balance and learn from this process of balancing.

Not all organizations face so many groups with the right to play a direct role in influencing policy, but they ignore those who are affected by what they do at their peril. This is equally true in other parts of the economy, where, increasingly, companies must respond to environmental or ethical demands from their stakeholders. A colleague tells a cautionary tale about a quarry, where the quarrying company consistently disregarded the protests of local inhabitants about the noise and dirt created by their lorries. However, when the company next applied for planning permission to expand, the local councillors, some of whom lived nearby and who had heard the protests, turned down the request.

The concept of stakeholders and the implications of their interests is a useful way of thinking about the wider public interest wherever you work. Application 10 is a process for considering who has a stake in what you do and what they might expect of you.

Application 10: Stakeholder analysis

The *purpose* of this activity is to identify those who have a stake in what you do and to help you to clarify the expectations of your company and the context in which you work. A stakeholder is *any individual or group who is affected by, or can affect, the future of your organization.* To be effective, you need to understand and respond to the expectations of the key stakeholders.

In doing this activity, it helps if you focus on a specific, new project or task. Think of a new development in which you are involved or are planning and ask yourself:

- Who has an interest in this development or might be affected by it?
- Who can affect its adoption or implementation?
- Who has expressed an opinion?
- Who ought to or might care about it?

It is important to consider both internal and external stakeholders, and to differentiate between subgroups if these have differing expectations. Consider future as well as present stakeholders. Using the columns below:

1 identify the individuals, and groups, you see as the key stakeholders
2 rank these stakeholders in your order of importance

Stakeholder	Expectations	Stakeholder	Expectations

4 *Analysis* Looking at the work you have done, consider the following questions in turn (it can be very helpful to do this with a colleague or friend—get them to quiz you on these issues to make sure that you are fully understanding the implications of your stakeholder analysis and map).

- How easy did you find it to identify expectations?

_____

_____

_____

- When did you last check if your perceptions are accurate/up to date?

  _____

- Did you find it hard to prioritize your list?

  _____

- What are the implications of your answers?

  _____

  _____

  _____

(Based on Aspinwall, *et al.*, 1992. p. 87–91)

You can take this exercise a stage further in Application 11 to consider what power these groups have as customers, clients or users now and in the future. This is especially important if you are planning a change.

Application 11: Micro-political mapping

Having identified all those individuals and groups who have some kind of stake in your organization, list their interests and their main sources of power. Note:

- their *orientation* in terms of positive support, neutrality or resistance
- their *power* to support or resist.

Place your stakeholders in the four quadrants shown:

- powerful and supportive
- powerful and resistant
- weak and supportive
- weak and resistant.

| | **Orientation** | |
Strong resistance	Neutral	Strong support
High p o w e r Low		

What does your picture look like? Specifically:

• Is there a critical mass of support necessary to implement the change?

_____

• Where do key individuals and groups appear?

_____

_____

• How might/should each group be treated to increase the likelihood of a successful change?

_____

_____

_____

_____

_____

Again it can be very helpful to do this step with a colleague or friend, and have them help you through these questions to ensure you have fully appraised the situation. Possession of the political map will not of itself make you an effective operator, but it will help you to avoid naïve errors.

For example:

• Can the powerful *supporters* be engaged to persuade the powerful *resisters* to become more supportive or at least reduce their resistance?
• Can those who are supportive but weak be empowered? For example, can groups in this quadrant be brought together to reduce their isolation and develop a mission or sense of identity? Can they realize their 'voice'?
• Can the weak *supporters* work on the weak *resisters*? Attempts by powerful supporters to persuade weak resisters may generate a sense of pressure or coercion and make things worse.
• Is understanding a problem for resisters? If so, how can understanding of the proposed change be increased?
• Have you gained any new insight into the effects of your proposals that mean you need to reconsider your ideas?

(Based on Aspinwall, *et al.*, 1992, pp.196–9)

Micro-political mapping is an especially good tool to use with a team of people to help in generating a shared perception of a particular situation. Such a team can create a lot of energy for itself in developing an agreed strategy or way forward. However, understanding the politics of accountability is not just of value for problem-solving purposes—important though that is, another important benefit is the learning that can come from holding oneself to account.

From accountability to learning

As policy in public service is ultimately decided by governments—national and local—there is always an important macro-political dimension. In the UK, there has been a major change towards grant-related funding with in-built monitoring processes to ensure that the money is spent as intended. A renewed emphasis on audits and quality control is apparent in many of the public services, including healthcare, the police, local government and education.

In schools, the sharp edge of the new accountability is to be found in the inspection process launched by the Education Act 1992. This Act develops a new agency—the Office for Standards in Education (OFSTED) to replace Her Majesty's Inspectorate (HMI). OFSTED's function is to inspect each school every four years to report on:

- the quality of the education provided by the school,
- the educational standards achieved by the school,
- whether the financial resources made available to the school are managed efficiently, and
- the spiritual, moral, social and cultural development of pupils at the school.

(OFSTED, 1994, p. 5)

The framework for inspection in *The Handbook for the Inspection of Schools* lays out the criteria against which inspectors are to make their judgements. Although these new inspection requirements processes do impose added burdens, some schools are finding ways to make the experience a developmental one, as the following case shows.

CASE: Wisewood Primary

Wisewood Primary School in Sheffield has just under 300 pupils, who are taught in 10 classes. It is not an 'inner city' school, but the majority of the children live in rented Council or Housing Association accommodation. About 40 per cent are entitled to free school meals—a reflection of the unemployment and hardship facing many of their families.

The headteacher and staff decided to volunteer for inspection before the formal process started in primary schools in the summer of 1994. This meant involving a local team of primary inspectors who had completed their OFSTED training and wanted to develop their skills in using the framework before tendering their services to schools. The Headeacher, Marie Lowe, stresses that

> ... in no way did this make the inspection feel any less real. I have talked to several heads who have been inspected since September and I can't find any difference in the nature of the experience.

In this case, a team of six inspectors were in the school for four days. During this time, as in all inspections, they carried out classroom observations, talked to pupils and looked at their work. All documentation was reviewed—policies and written procedures, curriculum and timetables, information sent to parents, school development plans, budgets, minutes of meetings, staff handbooks and job descriptions, the National Curriculum assessments, exam results and standardized tests for pupils. Inspectors also talked to the Headteacher and staff about their perceptions of what happens in the school and held a parents' meeting at which no members of staff were present. In addition, all parents were invited to speak to the inspectors individually if they wished. The findings of the inspection were reported verbally to the Headteacher and the school's senior management a week after the inspection and the publicly available written report was sent to the school within five weeks.

Although this is a dramatic intervention in the daily life of the school, the Headteacher speaks very positively of the experience. She acknowledges that the preparation period was particularly tiring:

> We had all the necessary evidence and documentation available but it wasn't always in the form that was needed. I worked late into the night in the time before the inspection getting things in order.

However, the feeling of sorting things was very satisfying. The imminence of the inspection encouraged the staff to discuss and clarify many issues, such as curriculum coordination roles and coherence and progression in children's learning. These matters had been discussed before many times, but the knowledge that they would now have to be justified to outsiders brought a particular urgency to their debates.

There was a cheering and last-minute piece of action by a group of parents. It had been agreed that the inspection team could have use of the parents' room. A group of parents thought the room was too shabby and decided that they would decorate it in the week before the inspection began. On the Friday evening, staff worked to put the room back together and mounted displays of the children's work to provide the finishing touches. The Head says that this felt almost celebratory and left everyone feeling that they had shared positively in the preparation.

Inspectors are not permitted to give any formative feedback during the inspection and it sometimes proved unnerving for staff to find them in their classrooms making notes of everything they observed. This tended to magnify any difficult moments and made the teachers very self-critical. However, the professional dimension was very important to the staff. They welcomed the fact that people who 'knew what to look for' and whose opinion they respected were carrying out the examination.

The Headteacher felt mainly positive during the week. However, when at an early stage of the verbal feedback, the inspectors identified areas for action that they felt needed attention, she went into a 'doom loop'. As Argyris describes, she did not ease into this, she zoomed into it (1991, p. 104) and was quite unable to hear the positive statements in the report. She remained in this state of gloom and apprehension until the final draft was read to the governors a week later, when she was surprised to find that it was generally very positive and that the areas for action were largely those already identified by the staff themselves.

The school set out to use the inspection for developmental purposes and it has already proved fruitful. As a result, the Headteacher feels that the staff are very committed to this year's school development plan. Discussions of the report's findings at a staff development day enabled new members of staff to quickly tune into the way the school works. The areas for action suggested that the school should 'continue to develop', 'put greater emphasis on' and 'tighten up and clarify' three different areas of their work. The staff had already decided that the matters covered in the first two of these judgements were to be the school's next priorities for action, but found it more difficult to accept the comments on the third area as they felt that the inspectors' perceptions were rather different from their own. However, they did not reject the judgement out of hand. They elected, first, to review the situation carefully and check that what they thought was happening was actually happening. Once they had reassured themselves that the breadth of reading experience provided in the school was broader than that observed by the inspectors, they began to look at how they could document and make more explicit what they do. They also recognized that they should not become entirely preoccupied with these particular issues, but continue to sustain and build on the many strengths identified in the report.

The formal inspection process is rather different to the advisory role previously played by this LEA. When asked how this impinged on the desire to use the process for development, the Headteacher replied that the crucial matter was in being able to accept and agree with the judgements. There were one or two comments in the report that the staff had felt were either 'not true' or 'not typical', for example, based on inappropriate activity in the classroom of a temporary supply teacher. These were the most difficult to respond to positively.

The Headteacher had also been surprised by the reaction of the school's governing body. It had taken the whole experience very calmly, placing much more emphasis and energy on the appointment of a new deputy headteacher. They had been very pleased with the report and had organized a barbecue to thank the staff 'for doing so well', but did not see themselves as key actors in any part of the process, despite all the new powers disposed to them by the Education Act.

Marie Lowe is glad that the inspection happened. She likes the inspection framework, which she sees as reflecting best practice. The school is now documenting its activities within the framework's requirements and building its planning around the report's findings. She has only one real reservation. The OFSTED document is the product of years of creative development, which it crystallizes. It provides a fairly tight framework within which to work and, thus, some stability and security for schools after a period of extreme turbulence. However:

> If the framework becomes dominant in our thinking and if the inspectors spend all their time inspecting, where will new ideas and creativity and the 'magic' come from in the future?

The issue of accountability can be a difficult one for many organizations at the best of times. Accountability processes, such as audits or evaluation, are often undertaken by outsiders or perhaps by one department on another. They are often seen as rather cold processes where evidence is gathered that may be used against you.

> Accountability has traditionally meant stewardship, particularly in respect of public trust. But ... it has come to mean that someone is about to have 'the blame' laid on him or her.
> (Guba and Lincoln, 1989, p. 256)

This makes it hard to accept the process or, as in the case study above, to seek out developmental experiences for all those involved. Too frequently accountability and development are seen to be at the opposite ends of a continuum:

accountability ⟵——————————————⟶ development

Sometimes, for example, we believe that exposing a sensitive or very new area of development to evaluation may destroy what we examine or break into an area where confidentiality is necessary. At other times, we regard an auditing process as something to be lived through and forgotten as quickly as possible. Sometimes both the organization and the auditors or assessors do little more than go through the required motions. However, at best, accountability and development are seen as complementary processes.

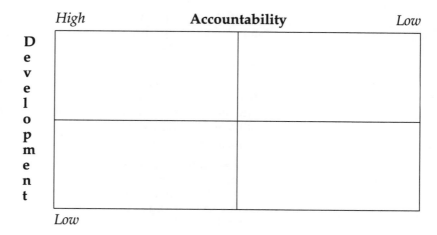

Figure 6.4   Accountability and Development matrix
(*Source:* Aspinwall, *et al.*, 1992, p. 96).

Can you place any recent processes of accountability on the matrix shown in Figure 6.4? Do they tend to cluster in one quadrant? What are the implications of this? You may be pleased with your conclusions. Learning to bring the two elements together in this way is a skill in itself. It is a part of the environmental scanning and feedback processes that are key to a learning company and intrinsic to approaches such as Total Quality Management (TQM) and Investors in People (IIP).

The professional approach to accountability

Professionals, both within and without public service, have traditionally been responsible for holding themselves to account, for the maintenance of quality work and for the self-policing of their profession. The Wisewood School case typifies the change in most walks of professional life, from doctors to lawyers, from police officers to financial advisers. The growing influence of 'user voice' or the 'empowerment of the customer' is fuelled by economic and social forces that have no respect for professional boundaries.

Some people will say, 'quite rightly so'—professionals being often seen as having abused their power. Professional knowledge can act as a shield, protecting people from recognizing any alternative way of knowing. One accusation takes this further, seeing professionals as 'capturing' their services, making them over to their own needs and purposes rather than to those they are supposed to serve. Such professionals, who not infrequently spout the service ethic in their defence, actually become unanswerable—except to themselves and their professional bodies (see Wilkinson and Pedler, 1995). This is a serious allegation, for it is the precise opposite of what is intended by 'being of public service'.

An additional consequence of strong professional identity can be the creation of barriers between different professions. Some years ago, a bemused teacher who had attended her first case conference about the needs of a pre-school child and her family reported:

> It was weird. There was the health visitor, the social worker, a community worker, the GP and myself. We all saw it from our own professional point of view. It felt as though we were talking about several different families. Then I realized Mrs S. herself wasn't even there.

Even some professionals fiercely question the concept. For example:

> I hate the idea of professionalism because it is a class system within the working environment, a way of being superior and at the same time submissive to exploitation.
>
> (Windsor, 1991, p. 5)

The stress on autonomy and self-judgement can lead to professionals being seen as particularly difficult to manage. They are not naturally compliant and often see their main loyalty as lying outside and beyond their employing organization:

> Engineering companies, R & D departments, accountancy sections and many public service departments are all dominated by people who very often have a strong professional view of their role . . .

However, far from this being an seen as an asset, it

> . . . may not be in accord with the managerial view on how these people can best be used as a resource.
>
> (Johnson and Scholes, 1993, p. 160)

Scholes discusses the characteristics of professionals as employees. They are independently minded, self-motivated, self-regulating and respectful of leadership—all, surely, desirable characteristics. However, they are also sometimes resistant to being 'managed'—requiring a high degree of autonomy—and may have a stronger allegiance to their profession than to their employer (1994, p. 6). In recent years, where the disadvantages of the latter characteristics have tended to overshadow the strengths of the former, considerable energy has often been put into using managerial strategies to pull professionals into line. It is not surprising that the imposition of managers over professionals used to using their own judgement (or having their own way) does not always go smoothly. The difficulties are compounded by the fact that, in many cases, the manager's role is to tighten or cut spending.

One management tool that many professionals have strongly resisted is that of performance-related pay (PRP). When the Government required 10 per cent of the pay rise in 1992/3 to be distributed in the form of PRP, one university elected to invite all academic staff to make their individual cases for receiving the payment. Most staff chose to ignore this request seeing it either as insulting or divisive. In one faculty a small number of staff did apply and received their bonuses. However, just before Christmas, each of their colleagues found some bank notes in an envelope on their desks with a note reading:

> Your share of the performance-related pay
> from your colleagues.

So, while accepting that some professionals (or even all professionals some of the time) exploit their position or themselves, this is not the whole picture. We rely on professionals for the most vital of services and this dependency will grow rather than diminish. Attempting to minimize the more difficult aspects of professional behaviour, we must also ask what happens to the strengths. Learning to manage with professionals is a crucial task for public service, and for most other organizations.

Application 12: Are you a professional?

In considering the part professionals play in work organizations, you might like to think about your own personal experience. How do you respond to the following questions?

1. Do you consider yourself to be a professional?

Yes ☐   No ☐

2. If either Yes or No, why do you say this? (What is your definition of 'professional' that makes you one or not?)

_____

_____

_____

3. How do you feel about this? (If you are *not* a professional, how does this make you feel about 'them'; if you *are* a professional, how do you feel about non-professionals?)

_____

_____

_____

In a 'knowledge age', more and more of us acquire and develop specialized know-how and information. We need to update ourselves constantly to stay abreast of development. We also find that this specialization makes it hard to explain the work to 'outsiders', and even to communicate with fellow professionals in another discipline. However, professionals have a lot in common with each other in terms of outlook on work and what sort of organization it is desirable to work for.

In their response to question 2 above, a group of hospital doctors came up with a long list, which included the following.

I am a professional because . . .

- *of the long training period I served*
- *the training is an 'apprenticeship'—there is a 'right way'*
- *I have a licence to practice (which can be taken away)*
- *of the need for professional 'refresher' training throughout my career*
- *of my membership of professional bodies—the British Medical Association, the Royal College of Psychiatrists and so on*
- *access to the profession is controlled and restricted by the professional bodies*
- *only my peers can judge my competence—through medical audit and so on*
- *I conform to a clear ethical code*
- *my commitment is to medicine, not to the particular hospital in which I work*
- *I am responsible for my own work and for no one else's*
- *medicine has a long history—it has become a profession over time*
- *my first responsibility is to the patient—I am judged on how well I do for that person.*

A group of NHS hospital managers were asked if they thought they were professionals and they were very mixed in their views—some thought they were and some did not. It was obvious when they looked at the doctors' list that they did not meet the strict criteria of *professional*—of restricted access to the profession, formal apprenticeship, licence to practice and so on. However, on less strict criteria, for example:

- possessing specialist knowledge and skills
- a constant need to update their knowledge and skills
- being competent and effective
- having ethical standards
- doing their work in a serious and 'professional' manner

they all felt they were professional workers—they were people who did a good job, subject to 'competence tests' and so on. Most importantly, they aspired to many of the professional freedoms and autonomy which they thought the doctors had. This point is critical because it illustrates what they look for in *their* organization and management.

4. Whether or not you see yourself as being a professional, check the following and tick all of the features you would like in your working situation:

- autonomy and independence—the right to use my own judgement ☐
- tenure—dismissal only on the grounds of 'unprofessional conduct' ☐
- career advancement—not necessarily in the same organization ☐
- to be managed by fellow professionals ☐
- to train the next generation to do my job—formally ☐
- to work in a flat organization with very few levels of hierarchy ☐
- to operate within professional codes of ethics and conduct ☐
- to have responsibility for and access to ongoing professional training ☐

How many did you tick? Most of them? If we want people to take a professional attitude to their work, these are the working conditions that will most encourage them to do that.

Now think about yourself as a *consumer* of professional services.

Application 13: Dealing with professionals

1. Which characteristics would you like to see your ideal professional embody?

_____

_____

_____

_____

_____

2. What would you like to be able to count on when you need professional help?

_____

_____

_____

_____

_____

3. How much are you prepared to take professional advice when it conflicts with your own perceptions of what you need?

_____

_____

_____

_____

_____

4. What would you like to be able to make a specific professional who is affecting your life do or stop doing?

_____

_____

_____

_____

_____

5. What part do you think professional groups and associations should play in society?

_____

_____

_____

_____

_____

6. Who has a right to influence professional behaviour and in what way?

_____

_____

_____

_____

_____

7. How well do your answers match with those in Application 12?

_____

_____

New models of accountability

Professional dominance has been considerably shaken and the balance of power has quite definitely shifted in the last few years. In a useful summary, Simkins draws together four models of accountability relevant to public services in the UK, shown in Table 6.1 (Simkins, 1992, p. 7).

Table 6.1   Simkins' four models of accountability

	Professional	Managerial	Political	Market
Key actors	Professionals	Managers	Representatives	Consumers
Influences factors	Peer review	Hierarchy	Governance	Choice
Success criteria	Good practice	Effectiveness and efficiency	Policy conformance	Competitive success

Each of these four models of accountability is rather different in its effects. In the Wisewood School case, a professional group chose to be held to account by outsiders, but by fellow-professional outsiders. This is important, because the teachers trusted the inspectors to know what to look for, but the process clearly has a strong *political* dimension, a *managerial* dimension (in the model of school management embodied in the inspection framework) and also a *market* one, as the pupils and parents were consulted as consumers.

No one likes losing power or the sense of control over one's destiny. Indeed, there has been considerable difficulty for many in accepting the new forms of accountability. This is not always entirely a bad thing. Would we be happy for professionals to substitute unquestioning policy conformance for the concept of good practice, for example?

In other situations, is it the insistence on taking only one perspective that causes the problem? How can a doctor who sees their professional duty as being to treat patients and a manager who needs to make cuts to balance the books and achieve efficiency begin to talk to one another if only one of these two standpoints is considered to be valid? What happens, who adjudicates, when there is no single or coherent consumer voice or, more seriously, where there is direct conflict between different users of the same service?

It is interesting to note that of the new forms of accountability, thinking of the users of a service as 'customers' has had perhaps the most favourable reception within the public sector. Surveys to discover what the customers or clients want or need are becoming almost commonplace. Yet, market accountability, too, has its own problems:

When told that people will always put quality above anything else in choosing a service, Rennie Fritchie, Chair of South and West Regional Health Authority, chides her colleagues with the experience of her grandmother:

> My grandmother always shopped at the Co-op. This was not because it was the cheapest, not because it was the best, nor because it was the nearest—it wasn't—but because it was *her* shop, where she got the 'divi.'. I can still remember her number. It was 609.

The Independent reported that a television programme for teenagers, *Byker Grove*, had been criticized by viewers for its gritty reality. However, when the Producer of the programme asked a group of 14 year-old girls what subjects they would like the programme to cover:

> ... teenage pregnancy and rape were the most popular, followed by eating disorders and death ... provided it was not Duncan's (one of the Grove's key characters).

> (Clarke, 1994)

Who are the customers here—the teenagers, their parents, the licence holders in general, the Government—who decides whose opinions are paramount?

Richards (1992) explains how the recent changes have created a 'new paradigm' in public service, replacing an earlier administrative orientation in which professional expertise was largely unchallenged.

Figure 6.5　The public administration paradigm

Figure 6.5 shows the traditional administered bureaucracy, with checks and balances designed to reduce the chance of abuse of power at the cost of being often slow-moving and inherently conservative.

An intermediate 'efficiency' approach seeks to make professionals accountable on the basis of managerial values using managers to try and control the hitherto autonomous professionals. This is shown in Figure 6.6.

Figure 6.6   The efficiency paradigm

With managers taking on the job of ensuring that policy is delivered, this intermediate paradigm appears more efficient. However, it does not take account of users/consumers, and it reduces the professional voice.

In the 'new paradigm', these forces are balanced, with managers fulfilling the essential negotiating, balancing role, holding the ring, as we can see in Figure 6.7.

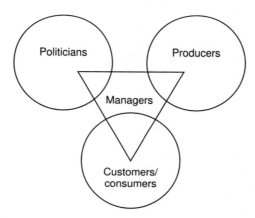

Figure 6.7   The new paradigm
(*Source:* Richards, 1992, pp. 9–28)

Richards notes that, in practice, the situation may not be as balanced as this suggests. Increasingly, producers/professionals are being pushed with the consumers into the area of micro-policy making, leaving the big decisions to the politicians.

Towards a new professionalism

These alternative forms of accountability break into the professionals' world and demand that they reconsider what they do. Despite (perhaps because of!) the discomfort, the balancing and blending of the elements of the four different models can enrich and enhance learning. This can be difficult as those losing power often feel vulnerable and defensive, while those gaining it may become overexcited in their desire to compensate for past weakness. However, it can work when the 'key actors' are able to respect and hear each other.

We think that some of the best examples of learning in the public sector are found where professionals consciously set out to examine their working practices and work together to improve what they do. Sometimes, as in the Wisewood School case, they use pre-existing externally devised processes. In other situations, they devise their own. In our next case study we look at just one example of this—a practice development unit (PDU) in a hospital. This PDU was consciously designed to promote interdisciplinary learning and to ensure the continuous improvement of professional practice.

CASE: The Practice Development Unit, Seacroft Hospital, Leeds

The Practice Development Unit, (PDU) is part of Seacroft Hospital, Leeds (now merging with St James). It sees itself as a logical extension of the nursing development units, which have developed in various parts of the country to provide centres of excellence and innovation in the practice of nursing.

The Unit is itself the result of an earlier merger between St Georges and Seacroft Hospitals, which brought staff from an institution catering for elderly, long-stay patients together with the Department of Medicine at Seacroft. This move required staff to work with more critically ill patients of all ages and in wards with a much more rapid turnover, a significant change in their function.

Not surprisingly this was not an easy process for staff, some of whom felt deskilled and lacking in confidence as a consequence. Hugo Mascie-Taylor, the Clinical Director, and Debbie Lee, the Patient Services Manager, decided to take active steps to ease the process and to build skills and confidence in staff through teamwork and the breaking down of professional barriers. A strong focus on the needs of patients would provide the unifying process.

The Unit was therefore designed from the outset to promote multidisciplinary working among all health professionals:

> Practice does not develop in isolation without teamwork and involvement from all professional disciplines and of course most importantly, the patient.

> (Practice Development Unit, 1994/5, p. 2)

Hence the choice of the word 'practice' rather than 'nursing' in the Unit's title.

The Unit comprises three wards, with physiotherapy, dietetics and occupational therapy also being ward-based to facilitate the provision of holistic, patient-focused care.

It is quite explicit about its essential components:

> Research and research-based practice are integral components. Staff are

encouraged to have a questioning attitude to what they do, and to identify and engage in practice-based research activity.

(Practice Development Unit, 1994/5, p. 2)

Turner stresses the need for an organization 'to be effective at continuing shared enquiry' if it is to be able 'repeatedly to set and resolve problems' and move beyond 'the competency trap' (1991, p. 4). This sense of learning through shared enquiry that is enriched by the crossing of professional boundaries comes over strongly from the staff of the Unit. The Unit also extends its links outside its boundaries, for example, maintaining close links with the Leeds Metropolitan University's Faculty of Health and Social Care.

In addition to the ongoing research, the clinical audit processes in the Unit require systematic and critical analysis of the quality of clinical care received by patients. One member of staff speaks of research being 'about finding the best way to do something' and an audit as 'finding out whether we're doing it'. The whole culture of the Unit is designed to promote a commitment to enquiry and staff recognize:

- the supportive environment
- a supportive management
- the availability of expertise
- constructive criticism

and

- respect between professions

as key factors underpinning the process of changing practice through research.

Innovation

Creative practice is encouraged and change for the better is accepted as an essential feature of development, which includes well-considered risk taking at all times.

Responsible risk taking is difficult in a hospital for obvious reasons—no one wants to encourage wild medical experiments—but, also because tight bureaucratic procedures discourage creativity.

Multidisciplinary teamwork

No one profession takes overall responsibility or leadership for practice development. Emphasis is placed on the benefits of sharing expertise and knowledge across professional boundaries in the pursuit of excellence in patient care.

A visit to the PDU confirms that the professional interaction is valued by everyone and seen as a definite bonus of working in the Unit.

We don't just talk about teamwork here, we really work as a team. We listen to each other and value our different perspectives, it helps everyone.

The need for multidisciplinary work comes from the recognition that patients need holistic therapeutic care. A practical outcome of the different professionals working together is *The Multidisciplinary Patient Assessment Booklet*. This is completed by:

> ... the primary nurse, consultant, admitting medical officer, senior house officer, physiotherapist, dietician, pharmacist, speech therapist, social worker, liaison nurse and any relevant others.

Patient empowerment

Patients are encouraged to be involved in decision making about their care and the PDU should be continually seeking ways of enabling them to participate more fully.

The Multidisciplinary Patient Assessment Booklet and other documents are held by each patient, who has to give permission before anyone reads them. The patient also contributes their own identification of problems and, after the nurse or therapist's contribution, an agreed summary is recorded to be used as the basis of the care plan. One valuable consequence of this process is that 'professionals have reduced their use of technical jargon enabling patients to understand their treatment more clearly' (Williams, George and Lowry, 1994, p. 29).

Staff empowerment

There is a workplace culture that delegates power downwards and encourages staff of all grades and disciplines to be involved in decision making.

Forums have been created within the Unit to provide maximum opportunity for everyone to make an input. Staff have their own learning contracts and are themselves encouraged to identify and develop areas for research and development.

Dissemination

> The PDU has an obligation to disseminate information regarding its work both within the organization, locally and nationally, in order to support the development of patient care.

Involvement in the dissemination of the work of the Unit has proved to be an empowering experience in itself. It is clear that individuals have gained a great deal from recording what they are doing and conveying their findings through conference papers and welcoming visitors to the Unit.

The general optimism within the Unit does not mean that there have been no casualties. Some staff have undoubtedly felt that they lost more than they gained in this process. But most have welcomed the changes, helped by the style of leadership explicitly identified as appropriate for the Unit. Specific professional background is not a criterion, but the clinical leader must create:

> a clinical climate which encourages and empowers nurses and therapists to be knowledgeable, reflective and autonomous practitioners who work

in harmony together ... (through) ... facilitating, coordinating, enabling, resourcing, providing a global view and vision.

(Practice Development Unit, 1994/5, p. 11)

Which is, of course, the type of leadership professionals prefer. The theme of balance is also vital. Staff are always faced with difficult choices—dilemmas about whether to give priority to *this* desirable aim or *that*, equally desirable, one. There are also always those routine, mundane, but essential daily tasks to be carried out. Discussing the way forward at a celebration of the PDU in 1994, its leader, Steve Page, recognized the factors that have to be held in balance if the team is to fulfil its purpose:

- day-to-day care and change and innovation
- innovation and consolidation
- practical work and academic work
- development and research
- professional orientation and service orientation
- pure quality and value for money
- open agenda and focused agenda
- independence and integration.

Although the overwhelming impression is of a group of people who are stimulated and energized by their task, no one expects the future to be easy, or wants it to be. The emphasis on personal autonomy, responsibility and innovation seems to be reaping a rich reward.

Some conclusions

The learning experiences of the PDU at Seacroft Hospital and Wisewood School illustrate what can be done by professional people at their best. Here we have public service staff who have looked to the future, set out to improve what they are doing and who are intent to share their learning with others. The sharing of good practice and new developments across and within public service organizations has been normal practice in the past and has been generally promoted by their local and regional tiers. It is to be hoped that, despite the new emphasis on competition within the public services, individuals and organizations will continue to share their learning to the benefit of the wider community in this way.

The small businesses and the big commercial companies that we looked at in earlier chapters operate to different purposes and expectations. After the one-way street of the 1980s, Judith Hunt, Chief Executive of the UK's Local Government Management Board, outlines three lessons that the private-sector managers of the 1990s could learn from the best of their public services colleagues:

One is a commitment to service that makes company motivational devices look trivial and shallow. The second is a capacity for local innovation based on multiple relations and partnership ... the third is a strong framework of propriety. Some of our strengths are in audit and the obligation to be accessible to the public with information.

(Interview in *The Observer*, 19 February 1995)

As we have seen, there is much that public services organizations can learn from private sector companies in terms of consumer awareness, a rapid responsiveness and flexibility to change. There are also important differences between public services and commercial organizations. The stories from public services are played out in a different context but are as encouraging and inspiring as any. The proper product of public services is to contribute to the public good and to a civilized society. Ultimately, this means making a contribution to the development of individuals and to social change. It is precisely because of the demands we make and the standards that we rightly expect from public services that best practice here has much to teach other companies concerned with ethics, accountability and with the further development of their professional services.

In the next chapter, we go on to look at another growing, but often poorly recognized, sector of the economy—the voluntary associations—that in the era of the 'enabling council' and cuts in public services funding, are more and more the partners of the statutory authorities in creating and maintaining public services. Again, they operate in somewhat different conditions and have different concerns. What do they have to teach us about the learning company?

References

Argyris, C. (1991) 'Teaching Smart People how to Learn', *Harvard Business Review* May/June, pp. 99–109.

Aspinwall, K., Simkins, T., Wilkinson, J. and McAuley, J. (1992) *Managing Evaluation in Education*, Routledge, London

Barber, M. (12 July 1994) 'A Right and Romantic Ideal', *The Independent on Sunday*

Clarke, S. (17 August 1994) *The Independent*

DoH (1994) *Draft Code of Conduct for Hospital Trust Boards*, HMSO, London

Elcock, H., 'Strategic Management' (1994) in Farnham, D. and Horton, S. *Managing the New Public Services*, Macmillan, London

Farnham, D. and Horton, S. (1994) *Managing the New Public Services*, Macmillan, London

Harrow, J. and Wilcocks, L. (1990) 'Public Service Management: Activities, Initiatives and Limits to Learning', *Journal of Management Studies*, 27 (3)

Johnson, G. and Scholes, K. (1993) *Exploring Corporate Strategy* (3rd ed.), Prentice-Hall, London

OFSTED (1994) *The Handbook for the Inspection of Schools*, HMSO, London

Pollitt, C. (1993) *Managerialism and The Public Services* (2nd ed.), Blackwell, Oxford

Pollitt, C. and Harrison, S. (1992) *Handbook of Public Service Management*, Blackwell, Oxford

Practice Development Unit (1994/5) *The Team Approach to Better Health: Practice Development Unit profile*, Department of Medicine, Seacroft Hospital, Leeds

Richards, S. (1992) *Who Defines the Public Good?: The consumer paradigm in public management*, Public Management Foundation, London

Scholes, K. (1994) *Strategic Management in Professional Service Organizations (PSOs): The finders, minders and grinders*, Sheffield Business School, Sheffield

Simkins, T. (1992) 'Policy, accountability and management: Perspectives on the implementation of reform', in Simkins, T., *et al.* (Eds) *Implementing Educational Reform: The early lessons*, Longman, Harlow

Stewart, J. (1989) 'In Search of a Curriculum for Management in the Public Sector', *Management Education and Development*, 20 (3), pp. 168–75

Turner, B. A. (1991) 'Rethinking Organizations: Organizational Learning in the Nineties', paper presented to EFMD Research Conference, ISIDA, Palermo

Wilkinson, D. and Pedler, M. (1995) 'Strategic Thinking in Public Service', in Garratt, B. (Ed.) *Developing Strategic Thought*, McGraw-Hill, Maidenhead

Williams, C., George, L. and Lowry, M. (1994) 'A Framework for Patient Assessment', *Nursing Standard*, 8 (38), June pp. 29–33

Windsor, S. (1991) *The Observer*, 19 May p. 5

7   Organizing for human service

The volunteer spirit is a vital sign of the health of a society. A 1991 Volunteer Centre UK survey estimated that some 23 million British adults had done some voluntary work in the previous 12 months. In the USA:

> ... with every second American adult serving as a volunteer in the non-profit sector and spending at least three hours a week in non-profit work, the non-profits are America's largest 'employer'.
> (Drucker, 1990, p. xiii)

Contributing through 'gift work' is a major individual and organizational activity and one that meets needs in the receiver *and* in the giver. The output or product of this huge 'industry' is of vital importance:

> Its product is a *changed human being*. The non-profit institutions are human-change agents. Their 'product' is a cured patient, a child that learns, a young man or woman grown into a self-respecting adult; a changed human life altogether.
> (Drucker, 1990, p. xiv)

The voluntary sector is growing in size and importance. Leading, organizing and managing for the best result at the least cost is as critical here as elsewhere. And why not?

Volunteering began, perhaps, with charity as an aspect of the spiritual life. Churches urged their members to give for the sake of their souls—for the upkeep of buildings, to run hospitals and to relieve suffering. In Britain, the dissolution of the monasteries in the sixteenth century brought about a secularization of charity, with schools and almshouses being run by parishes and other local authorities. Voluntary societies boomed in Victorian times of self-help. Housing trusts, health and educational charities and those for the alleviation of poverty flourished alongside the self-educational literary and philosophical societies and the mechanics' institutes, while the building societies and insurance companies were founded on the same principles of mutual aid and protection.

Many charities, then and now, have their origins in the discovery of a new need and are set up to provide a new service. A recent example is the women's aid movement which, in the 1970s, exposed hitherto hidden domestic violence and provided local refuges for battered women. Voluntary organization can be a force for social change, where self-help, voluntary action and campaigning in response to an unmet need eventually lead statutory authorities to recognize and provide for that need. As well as dealing with the immediate need, such action can effect big changes in public opinion and create new employment.

The sector is enormously varied and hard to define. One estimate is that there are 250 000 charities in England and Wales, with an annual turnover of £12.5 billion. Voluntary organizations range from the small and local—self-help groups, local history or conservation societies, neighbourhood watch groups and so on—to the huge and national—Age Concern in the UK alone has over 250 000 regular volunteers. Some, such as the Red Cross or Greenpeace, are international and operate on a worldwide basis. Taken together, they define so many aspects of what we mean by society—caring for the elderly, children, the countryside or the inner city, animal welfare, world poverty, homelessness, historic buildings, cancer research ... the list is virtually endless.

One way of describing the 'voluntaries' is to see them in three groups:

- large, professional organizations with growing incomes based on sophisticated fundraising and service contracting
- middle-level organizations, which are a mixture of pro-fessional and volunteer staff and are rather like small businesses concerned for their 'market niche'
- the vast majority, only some of which are registered charities, who form the local social economy of self-help/ mutual aid groups and cooperatives.

Another describes them by function (the following analysis is based on Handy, 1988, pp. 10–13).

- *Mutual support* Organizations that exist to put people of similar needs or enthusiasms in touch with each other to give companionship, help and advice. Many voluntary organizations start here with the discovery of a new need— for example, to support people with a particular illness or problem. Many mutual support groups are concerned with leisure or recreation. A study of leisure interest groups in Kingswood, Surrey, found that there were 300 groups involving 28 000 people in a population of 85 000. While many of these groups are small and local, others, such as the Royal Society for the Protection of Birds and the National Trust, measure their membership in millions.

- *Service delivery* Organizations that exist to provide services to those in need, for example, Arthritis Care, MIND (mental health), OXFAM (famine and poverty relief), Royal National Institute for the Blind. These service delivery organizations are often the biggest, employing professional core staff, sometimes in quite large numbers—Barnardo's, for example, employs some 4600 paid staff.

- *Campaigning* Organizations that exist to articulate a particular need or to lobby for a cause. This category includes some high-profile organizations, such as the Campaign for Nuclear Disarmament (CND) and Greenpeace. Campaigning organizations are often led by charismatic figures and, like mutual support groups, tend to be administered rather than managed.

But, no three-fold classification can absorb the variety of the voluntary sector. Many service delivery organizations have a campaigning aspect, for example, acting as pressure groups for a particular need as well as providing services to those in need. Others are engaged in research and publication as a way of achieving their goals. Some have become so recognized in their fields that governments, political parties and others rely on them for information that would otherwise not exist.

Neither 'private' nor 'public'—not controlled by the State nor listed on the Stock Market—who owns these not-for-profit organizations? In the UK, the growing significance of this sector of the economy goes largely unrecognized, but in France (and now the EU) they call it 'l'economie sociale', and it is acknowledged in Sweden as the 'third sector'. This is much more satisfactory than P. Drucker's negative 'non-profit sector', with its implications that, not only is profit the norm, but that it is in the profit-making sector that real organizations and management exist—a view still reflected in most UK and USA textbooks. The 'voluntary sector' is not particularly satisfactory, with its suggestions of marginality, amateurism and suspicions of 'do-goodism'. However, it is in other ways a very positive term and, as the one most in currency, it will have to do here.

Managing with volunteers

In giving, many volunteers gain a great deal for themselves. The Victorian 'do-gooding' image of middle-class folk giving hand-outs to the poor clings on stubbornly in some quarters. However, this is usually far from the reality, although its re-emergence on the streets of London and other big cities is one of the signs of our times. The modern State with its stress on equality of treatment, universal benefits and individual rights has set out to replace the Victorian volunteers with a great deal of success and genuine social progress. In recent years, many parts of this modern State have been subjected to a severe re-examination, especially from those who have blamed it for creating a 'dependency culture'. Over the twentieth century as a whole, we seem to have experienced a loss of community and an increasing fragmentation in our personal and social lives, as discussed in Chapter 1. This is the backcloth to the current emergence of the voluntary organizations as 'l'economie sociale'.

Many small voluntary organizations do not need managing, except in the administrative sense of the society's secretary and treasurer. Indeed, many are anti-management, in the sense of 'being managed'—something members, perhaps, have far too much of in other aspects of their lives. However, it is the basis of the volunteer worker's motivation that makes the business of management and organization problematic for many voluntary organizations.

Most managing is based, at least at bottom, on a 'cash nexus' in the relationship between manager and managed, rather than on a voluntary giving. Much of what we now call 'human resources management' has long been concerned with *how to motivate* people—from the outside as it were. Voluntary organizations do not have that problem—their workers come ready fired up from the inside.

> Home-Start provides friendship and informal support for parents, usually mothers, of children under school age. It was started in the early 1970s by Margaret Harrison, who noticed the isolation of many mothers and the deleterious effects of this on their morale and that of their families. From a local group in Leicester, Home-Start has grown to be a nationwide association with some 150 groups in the UK and branches in Europe and Australia.
>
> Anyone can have a Home-Start visitor. Requests must come from the parent—the only question is whether or not they need more specialized or professional help. Volunteers are given training and may only befriend one family at a time. One volunteer asked her local organizer for a new family; 'Have you

finished with Mrs _____ ?', she was asked. 'Oh, she's a friend now,' said the volunteer, 'she doesn't count'.

People who have Home-Start visitors, frequently become volunteer visitors themselves.

This sort of help can't be provided by professionals or paid workers. The paid person acts from different motives, works under staff conditions and is differently accountable. Not being paid for the work that you do changes your relationship to those you are serving (and also with your 'employer' as discussed below). If 'work is love made visible' (Gibran, 1926, p. 35), then perhaps voluntary work enables this self-expression without money getting in the way. Socially, as Drucker has pointed out, voluntary work is where many people get their sense of community, their sense of purpose and direction:

> Again and again when ... I ask 'Why are you willing to give up all this time when you are already working hard in your paid job?' ... I get the same answer, ' Because here I know what I am doing. Here I contribute. Here I am a member of a community.'
>
> (1990, p. xviii)

Current challenges

Volunteer effort—both in terms of funds and labour—is the 'added value' provided by voluntary service delivery organizations and it is what gives them their distinctive energy and contribution. This special power and resource needs to be safeguarded and managed. Demographic changes, especially an ageing population, mean that welfare services delivered by paid professionals become more and more expensive to operate. This increases the pressures for alternative provision, and the voluntary sector is the first port of call for many hard-pressed local authorities and Government agencies. Despite an estimated 6 million 'involuntary carers' (1984 General Household Survey), the Royal Commission on Citizenship found in 1990 that many UK public services are already heavily dependent on volunteers, and warned of the 'danger in an over-reliance on voluntary efforts'.

These pressures are readily apparent in the field. Age Concern has turned down requests from local authorities to substitute volunteers for paid staff; Arthritis Care decided not to get involved in contracting and the British Red Cross, whose 100 000 volunteers put in 5 million hours per year at an estimated value to the community of £24 million, would not use staff to act as strike breakers. The Red Cross's recent experience shows the tension between becoming more professional and successful, for example, in respect of fundraising, while showing a decline in terms of volunteers.

> Founded in Switzerland some 125 years ago, the Red Cross is the 'best known, but least understood' charity in terms of what it does—residential homes, community care, hospital loan services as well as disaster relief. Some 90 independent branches supported by 1500 paid staff form what is essentially a volunteer service. However, in recent years, while innovative fundraising has lifted income to £70 million from £40 million in 1989, at the same time, volunteer numbers have dropped from 200 000 ten years ago. This reflects social trends, but the society recognizes that it must be 'cleverer about the way we market our services to volunteers'. Maintaining key traditions, the Red Cross is adapting to changing circumstances by using the modern language of management and rediscovering its vision and values as well as its unique selling point—a focus on emergencies.
>
> (*The Independent*, 26 January 1995)

The voluntary sector now underpins much State or public provision:

> Today voluntary organizations are relatively fashionable, by which I mean that since the end of the Second World War the fortunes of voluntary organizations have fluctuated. A fully-fledged cradle-to-grave Welfare State would have found little room for voluntary organizations. At the other end of the spectrum a privatised welfare system would change the nature of voluntary bodies, driving them to become ever more competitive bidders for contracts to care for the elderly, children, the countryside or the inner city. Voluntary organizations have been subject to many of the same pulls and pushes that have affected industry and other sectors of society over the past forty years.
>
> (Hinton, 1988, p. vii)

As a result of demographic shifts and changing times, the increase in demand for their services coming from local authorities and Government agencies is prompting major organizational change in the voluntary service 'companies' just as much as in their commercial cousins. New relationships with statutory authorities, multi-agency working with provider partners, changing public images (such as Barnardo's, which is now the UK's 'biggest child care agency'), the need for quality inspections and audits, all fuel an organizational imperative to learn quickly and transfer this knowledge from one part to another.

For these, often big, organizations, service delivery means that managing scarce human resources, both paid and voluntary, is an increasingly absorbing issue. Some of the particular problems of management and organization are:

- How can we transform ourselves to meet the demands of the time without losing our sense of history and values?
- How can we raise funds in *competition* with other voluntary organizations and also *cooperate* in spending with these same societies to deliver coordinated services?
- Should we become more involved in partnerships—with other voluntary bodies, public services and the business community?
- Do the changes required mean that we should get involved in mergers, acquisitions, dispersals and restructurings in a way not dissimilar to that of some private-sector companies?
- Who should determine policy? Trustees, Government, funders, professional staff or volunteers?
- How can volunteer staff be involved in, and contribute to, policy formation?
- What quality of services is delivered by volunteers, compared with paid staff?
- What skills will we need in the future? How can we organize to develop these? What joint learning and development needs do we have with other organizations?

Meeting the challenges

These are some of the problems that form the agenda for the voluntary sector learning company. However, these same problems are the source of great opportunity for the responsive voluntary. As a result of the challenges raised by changing times, many service providers are growing rapidly in terms of full-time staff and turnover, and are becoming better at business and management. Take, for example, Age Concern.

Much of the day care offered to old people in the UK, especially the mentally frail, is provided by local Age Concern groups, using a mix of paid and voluntary workers in close liaison with health and social services professionals. With 250 000 regular volunteers, over 11 000 people are involved in managing, either as trustees of local independent groups or directly in local operations.

As with other voluntaries, Age Concern is feeling the impact of major change, with old traditions needing to adapt to the efficiency, accountability and professionalism now required. The Community Care legislation of the early 1990s creates opportunities to offer local services to elderly people that are well beyond the traditional day care, advice and information provided by local groups.

Increasingly, Age Concern organizations are operating a variety of 'care' services on a contractual basis. These include visiting schemes, day care services and sometimes home care services (previously run by local authorities as home help services). Some groups operate nursing and residential homes on a contractual basis. These businesses have the usual management and organizational problems. However, few people in Age Concern have received management training or have many connections with the world of business. This is beginning to change; training opportunites are improving and outside connections are growing as Age Concern seeks to be more imaginative, innovative and responsive.

(Hunt, 1991)

A dilemma facing Age Concern, and others like them, is whether or not they should compete for public contracts with all the inherent dangers of public service incorporation, or should remain an independent, campaigning organization, relying on grants and donations.

Those voluntaries who have chosen the former route have become more business-like, more concerned with costs and standards and have appointed professionals rather than users to their boards. Local authorities, themselves increasingly strapped for cash and faced with escalating demands, have demanded 'more for less' and imposed quality standards and other requirements in their contracts. The 'enabling Council' has turned more and more to the voluntary sector as the direct service provider, thus making voluntary organizations increasingly an arm of the authority.

While some of these changes show obvious benefits, there is a danger of losing the volunteer and user focus that is the lifeblood of campaigning and fundraising. For this reason and from fear of becoming dependent, some groups have taken policy decisions not to accept contracts. However, if they do not accept contracts or are slow to adapt to the new contract culture, will they be able to maintain their income?

For voluntaries, a continual negotiation of their autonomy and dependence seems inevitable:

> ... all forms of resource acquisition, competition and collaboration are essentially about the negotiation of interdependence. Autonomy is not given: it is struggled for within the inevitable constraints of a shifting environment ... for the great majority of voluntary organizations ... strategic issues involve different ways of negotiating their interdependence .... The generic skills and challenges of managing expansion and contraction, evaluating performance, balancing the demands of different stakeholders, networking and forming alliances across sectoral boundaries, managing values issues and conflicts, remain as important as ever.
>
> (Batsleer and Paton, 1993, in Jarman, 1994, pp. 20 and 21)

To look at how the sector is meeting such challenges, here is a case study of Barnardo's, the UK's largest and best-known voluntary childcare organization, with international offices in Ireland, Australia and New Zealand. Among its ambitions, Barnardo's has adopted the aspiration to become a learning organization

CASE: Barnardo's

Dr Barnardo's. The very name conjures up the image of orphaned children. Big, grey, residential mansions reeking of carbolic, polish and yesterday's cabbage. Of *papier mâché* collection boxes and Dickensian images of round-eyed street urchins.

(*The Guardian*, 19 October 1988)

It is now 128 years since Irish immigrant Dr Thomas John Barnardo founded the organization to care for abandoned children on the streets of London. The orphanages are long gone now and have been replaced by more diverse work, including community-based support for disadvantaged or disabled young people, education and employment projects, fostering and adoption for children needing families, day care and parenting programmes for families with young children. Through its anti-poverty strategy, Barnardo's also actively campaigns for change on behalf of children and poor families.

With its 165 childcare projects involving 4600 paid staff and some 2600 volunteers, Barnardo's provides services for 22 000 children. Its fundraising is supported by a further 100 000 volunteers who support house-to-house campaigning and other fundraising activities. Barnardo's services include working with:

* homeless young people, for example, young Asian women in Birmingham
* young offenders, including those who sexually abuse other children
* families affected by HIV/AIDS
* a Lake District holiday centre for severely disabled young people
* Dr B's restaurants, offering good food and job training for young people with learning disabilities.

Despite the social and welfare advances of the twentieth century, Barnardo's has never been more necessary than today. It is experiencing rapid growth and change—the 1993/4 income of £77 million is an increase of more than 50 per cent over the last 3 years.

Learning to keep pace with change ...

Dr Barnardo's vision, purpose and Christian values have remained crucial to the organization throughout its history. Many staff and volunteers join because of these values. Commitment is a two-way street and Barnardo's must give it back to its people. In order to give disadvantaged young children a sense of belonging, Barnardo's needs also to create that binding and belonging within the organization.

In October 1988, the 'Dr' from Barnardo's dropped into history. Not achieved without pain, this move is emblematic of the changing times. Moving from a sentimental, Victorian image to today's more radical mission—'working together to challenge disadvantage and create new opportunities'—keeps Barnardo's up to date while hanging on to the stability, reliability and recognition value of the name.

Keeping the faith

Another critical challenge has been to Barnardo's values. How can a Christian-based organization adapt to a multifaith and multicultural society? In 1991, Barnardo's reviewed and revised its Christian basis to this end. Barnardo's stated values might now be embraced by any humanist:

- respecting the unique worth of every person
- encouraging people to fulfil their potential
- working with hope
- exercising responsible stewardship

but are backed by an ethical creed that is 'derived' from its Christian tradition, enshrined in its Articles of Association and which it now intends should be 'enriched' by other faiths. Today, at least two-thirds of Barnardo's Council members and all four National Directors must still formally affirm their Christianity, although it is theoretically possible for a Sikh, say, to become a Divisional Director. Significant as these changes are, they still leave a situation that, technically at least, could be said to infringe the thoroughgoing equal opportunities policy required of an organization the *raison d'être* of which is working against discrimination, disadvantage, disability.

Much energy and angst goes into such changes. 'Knee-deep in Foundation Statements' (Jarman, 1994) that are the voluntaries' greatest sources of strength, these same values throw out a shadow side. From a managerial perspective, any unpleasant but normal managerial action, such as cutting a budget, closing a project, disciplining a person, making someone redundant, can be done in accordance with the basis and values, principles and standards of the organization. They can also be interpeted by staff as offending one or more of these high principles and may then be cited in memos and protests by upset staff members and other interested parties. Such no-win situations with their attendant grief and anger are to be found in the shadow of high standards.

Working in partnership with statutory authorities

One of the main challenges with which Barnardo's struggles—like many other voluntary service providers—is the issue of contracting with local authorities to provide various children's services. The ability to respond to this 'opportunity' provides potential for growth and development of the organization. While this might allow for a great expansion in work, it also presents the organization with a dilemma: Barnardo's does not exist to subsidize statutory responsibilities, as for example, under the Children's Act 1989. Yet, the boundaries between what is and what is not statutory are not clear, and local authorities are, at best, in 'no growth' situations. Should Barnardo's use its precious voluntary resources to make up for shortfalls in local authority spending or ensure that they are available to be diverted towards Barnardo's purposes?

Like any other organization, Barnardo's has limited resources in terms of what it can do. It cannot be all things to all people; it must prioritize and change these priorities over time. If it takes on a new field of work—HIV and AIDS for example—something else may have to be dropped. The Victorian desire to 'do good' becomes the modern question 'What unique added value can Barnardo's bring to this particular situation?'. This usually turns on the resources it brings as a national voluntary organization—its strength and tradition of volunteers, relevant professional skills and expertise in working with children and young people, as well as funding.

As a result of many influences, including Government policy, local authorities are providing fewer direct services and becoming 'enabling councils'—commissioning and purchasing work from a variety of public, private and voluntary sector organizations. An example of this was a recent request from Manchester Social Services to talk to interested charities about 'leaving care work' for young people.

Barnardo's North West was keen to work in Manchester where it previously had not had a presence. Initially there was another dilemma: should Barnardo's inform other major voluntaries—potentially its competitors—such as the Children's Society and NCH Action for Children of its interests? Barnardo's decided to talk to the others about its plans. It was able to stay in the discussion and, therefore, influence and shape the service, because the organization was able to put in some voluntary income. Not all societies can do this and it gives Barnardo's considerable bargaining power in such situations. The outcome is a mutually acceptable deal on a service-level agreement between Manchester Social Services Department and Barnardo's as the main partner with the other charities considering their role in the provision of specialist services that will enhance the agreed service.

Cooperation and competition

This example illustrates the interdependent relationship Barnardo's has with other voluntaries in the field of childcare and work with young people. The theme is of partnership, cooperation and collaboration, yet it also raises issues of competition—

of one voluntary organization bidding for work against another in a market-type economy. In that situation, the parties want to share ideas and experiences fully, but may also be concerned that these ideas might be 'pinched' and a competitive advantage gained.

But if you do collaborate—and many new projects involve multi-agency working—who leads the project? Who employs the staff? Who recruits, trains and supervises them? As well as dealing with other national charities, there is an especially great need here to protect the small, local charity that may have put great energy and vision into the project to get it started and then runs the risk of seeing it taken over by the big, professional charity.

To help with these situations, the National Council for Voluntary Child Care Organizations (NCVCCO) in the North West has proposed a set of principles for working in the developing contract culture. These include:

- all organizational activity should be driven by the needs of children and their families, not organizational self-interest
- contracting should be based on openness not secrecy, collaboration not competition
- positive action is needed to support the survival and flourishing of small voluntary organizations
- voluntary organizations should work together to influence the way local authorities behave to ensure relationships in the contract culture are built on meeting children's needs and on developing the extent and range of services to children.

These hopeful, sensible principles are described as 'naïve' by Tim Brown, Director of Personal Services, St Helens, who feels that the voluntary organizations need to accept that some form of competition is an explicit part of the contract culture rather than seeking to form 'a cosy cartel'. Nevertheless, Barnardo's starting point is:

> ... that only a wholly collaborative effort at a local level, particularly including those who live in the very conditions we seek to affect, will ever bring real change.
>
> (Jarman, 1994, p. 3).

Learning from projects and operations

Such operational conditions mean that Barnardo's needs to learn quickly in order to maintain itself in the field and continue to develop as an organization. When a new project is set up, Barnardo's three internal departments—Appeals, Child Care and Financial and Corporate Services—must work together to make the project a success. Fundraising activities at both local and national level support this, from local Barnardo's helpers' groups to grand charity operas, from sponsored walks to cycle rides, coffee mornings and so on. A national network of shops selling donated goods provides additional funds.

At the same time, the Child Care Department will develop

volunteering to support the project's services, perhaps through a volunteer organizer (VO)—a paid staff member—recruiting, training, deploying and supervizing local volunteers. Child Care staff, professionally qualified in social work, or for certain projects in teaching or youth work, train and supervise the VOs, who may be full- or part-time. Much investment goes into the training of volunteers, who typically receive six half-day sessions across a range of childcare issues, from child protection to working with violence. In return, volunteers from all walks of life, recruited from colleges, schools, local groups, invariably give great commitment to the work. Some volunteers are short-term, for a few weeks, such as on a summer playscheme, others may be the long-term visitors of a child with severe learning disabilities, week after week, year after year.

Because all projects reflect local needs and each develops its own procedures, there is a great need to share best practice. Barnardo's North West has been bringing its VOs together to share learning and develop good practice and procedures across its projects. It has also brought volunteers together by arranging Sunday conferences to learn more about the work of the organization outside of their particular project. The issue of qualifications for volunteers is one that Barnardo's is considering nationally, and one project has a pilot scheme to look at the value of NVQs for volunteers.

Learning in the learning company
The question of how to collect and share learning from projects is not confined to local efforts. A 1991 national working party report, 'Moving Forward' considered the difficult issue of priorities in deciding what services Barnardo's should provide and how. It regrouped existing work in five categories, and set up its 'Agenda for Action'—three areas where it felt the organization could achieve an impact, locally and nationally, namely homelessness, HIV/AIDS and child sexual abuse. It also looked at the organizational structures necessary to deliver effective local services. With the aim of achieving more local control and responsiveness, the 'key roles' played by project leaders and assistant divisional directors were examined. Project leaders were given more power to conduct their projects flexibly as local cost centres. Previously centralized support services, such as personnel and publicity, were devolved as part of the effort to make the organization more locally responsive.

At the level above the project leaders, the assistant divisional directors (ADDs) have assumed a more strategic role in the management of their divisions and in leading the development of policy and practice in the organization. The aim has been to encourage delegation to project leaders and to release ADDs from much of the operational management of projects. The intention is that each ADD should have line management responsibility for seven or eight projects, rather than the five they formerly had, to allow them to develop new services and to work more strategically.

New 'lead roles', dealing with the core categories of Barnardo's work plus the 'Agenda for Action', involve ADDs meeting with colleagues as part of a national group with the responsible lead officer from the organization's Policy and Development Unit. This brings together experience from the different divisions to influence the development of policy and practice within the organization. It also helps determine where Barnardo's should be campaigning externally and seeking to influence social policy. The usefulness of these lead roles, in spreading and sharing learning from the divisions as part of the development of national strategy, has been such that they are in danger of being over-relied upon:

> Papers coming to the national Child Care Management Meeting on policy matters frequently identify a lead role for an ADD ... for example, Complaints, Volunteers, Child Protection. There are now 14 of them—to share amongst 4 ADDs in Divisions.

New colleges of society?

> If you want an exciting, developing and changing organization, look for one where the individuals are themselves encouraged to be exciting, developing and changing.
>
> (Handy, 1998, quoted in Hayes, 1991, p. 82)

Barnardo's works with high levels of commitment; taken and given. As elsewhere, commitment from the organization can no longer include a job for life, and this places greater importance on the quality of working relationships in which people learn from and take responsibilities for each other. Unless work in Barnardo's is a learning experience, the organization will not be able to keep up with the demands from those it seeks to care for, the interests of its varied stakeholders and the volatility and precariousness of the contract culture.

But this learning is not just for the organization, important though that is. Working with Barnardo's—as a paid staff member, as a volunteer or as one receiving a caring service—must in itself be a 'value-adding' process. 'Working together to challenge disadvantage and create opportunity' means nothing if those involved do not learn and develop. Here lies Barnardo's chance to join in Handy's uplifting vision:

> Could the bigger voluntary organizations become the new colleges of society, providing new skills, new horizons and new lives for its citizens, many of whom feel de-skilled by their earlier experiences of life? Should voluntary organizations recognize that they exist at least as much for their workers as for their clients and turn that to a positive advantage? Might they then not discover that organizations can enable people as well as use them? Might they then not learn to run themselves like an association rather than a factory, a partnership of like-minded people rather than a hierarchy of human resources?
>
> (1988, p. 161)

Note: This case is based on conversations with Sue Hayes, North West Divisional Director of Barnardo's, and draws on her unpublished MSc Dissertation, 'Excursions into Learning in the Voluntary Sector', Manchester Metropolitan University, June 1991.

Participation in policy making

Any organization like Barnardo's or Age Concern, that is centrally concerned with retaining the energies and enthusiasms of its staff and volunteers, has a lot of stakeholders. In Chapter 6 we discussed how the existence of multiple, and sometimes competing, stakeholders is one of the defining characteristics of most public services companies. In the voluntary sector, this aspect is magnified still further, and the demands of any one stakeholder cannot be put above those of the others. Donors, volunteers, paid staff, overseas partners, sponsoring bodies such as churches, project and campaign partners, Government agencies and, of course, the individual recipients of services are just part of the list for a national organization.

Finding means of involving this myriad of people and organizations in policy-making processes is a critical task for the learning company in the voluntary sector. Application 14 gives an example of how this can be done, together with a case illustration from the annual volunteer conference of a world poverty and development charity.

Application 14: Making priority choices

One of the problems in seeking to manage responsively and shape policy from the views of members or staff is finding a way to cope with the variety and volume of ideas that come up. After having taken the apparently bold step of asking instead of telling, many a well-meaning democrat has come unstuck when faced with an avalanche of ideas and competing priorities. The results of such consultations can be disappointing, or even damaging, if the leaders retreat in the face of too much data.

One simple and practical approach to choosing priorities from a mass of data and opinions is known as nominal group technique (NGT). There are many similar techniques, some of them using questionnaires and computers, such as Priority Search, but NGT is a method which can be done with paper and pens with everyone in the same room.

Use this method for prioritizing, ranking or voting on a list of items. In a face-to-face group, you can tackle up to about 50 items in a group of 2 to 25 members. It is possible to deal indirectly with much larger groups using, for example, a series of postal questionnaires or by holding a conference of representatives.

Step 1. Question: What is the question or issue on which you want to consult and make priority decisions?

(The technique works by generating a list of responses, options or possibilities around a particular question, such as 'Which development projects should we pursue over the next three to five years?' or 'How could we improve the way in which our service is delivered?' or 'How can we evaluate the usefulness of our work in country X?')

Step 2. Responses: Identify all possible responses to the question or issue.

(This can be done in a variety of ways—by collecting points from a group discussion, by brainstorming a list of responses, from an analysis of reports or surveys. If you are working with a small group in the room, you can ask everyone to write down their thoughts and then write them all up on the board. If you are dealing more indirectly with the whole company you can ask people to write in or send E-mail messages to a Bulletin Board. You could also send out a simple questionnaire.)

Step 3. List Items: Publish a list of numbered items.

(If you are working face-to-face, discuss and create an agreed list on flipcharts. Cut out duplicates and combine similar items to arrive at a list that everyone understands. A list of 20 or 30 items is usually enough. If you are working with the whole company or more indirectly, use a group of representatives to create the list which can then be sent out to all members as a questionnaire or checklist.)

Step 4. Rank Items: Ask members to rank the items.

(Ask each person to rank their priorities from the list presented. With 10 or 12 items, 5 priority choices per person might be appropriate; with 20 or more items, 10 choices will give a better picture.

Each person then chooses their 5 or 10 priorities and ranks them, giving 5 (10) points to their first priority and 1 point to their fifth (tenth). Again, this can be done face-to-face or via a questionnaire.)

Step 5. Tally the Rankings: Collect all members' rankings and aggregate them.

(In a face-to-face group, write members' names along the top of a flipchart and items down the left-hand side. Rule off to create a grid and score by asking each person to give their points allocation. Add up the score for each item—the highest number of points giving the top priority and so on. In a whole-company process, questionnaires or representative group scores are collated and published.)

Although this *sounds* a complicated process, it isn't. It's very simple if you take it step by step, and it can be very cheering to a group of people, first, in producing a long list of interesting and exciting choices, and then in accomplishing the difficult task of choosing among them.

An illustration of NGT in use

At the annual volunteer conference of an organization concerned with world poverty and development, delegates were asked, 'In what ways should the Society change over the next three years?' A list of 26 items was established from the 112 ideas submitted, and, on the second day of the conference, delegates formed into eight groups to agree on a ranking for the ten they considered most important.

The 26 items were:

1. allocate more funds to emergency aid in the developing world
2. use our research and publications to change IMF and the World Bank policies
3. change the internal structure of the organization to make decision making easier
4. put more effort into sponsoring fair trade—both overseas and in the UK
5. more emphasis on spirituality as well as material aid
6. reduce the number of committees by half
7. become more of a development agency, offering expertise as well as money
8. concentrate more and use more imaginative methods for fundraising
9. lobby our own Government for an increased allocation of overseas aid
10. recruit more young people
11. become less paternalistic, more empowering in style
12. increase our research output
13. cut down on the number of projects and focus priorities more
14. concentrate on education about the developing world in the UK
15. combat 'compassion fatigue' by being more adventurous and exciting
16. make management less 'white, male and middle-aged'
17. recruit more black and Asian volunteers
18. share resources and campaigns with other agencies like ourselves
19. improve the relationship between head office and the regions
20. start the debate on a sustainable world economy
21. put more faith in volunteers' ideas
22. campaign for the reform of corrupt governments in the developing world
23. base new projects on better research and evaluation evidence
24. start an educational representatives scheme to carry the message to schools and colleges
25. ensure that all offices and premises have good access for the disabled
26. establish a limit for the amount of funding from Government

The rankings were then plotted and the top ten priorities established as follows.

Item	A	B	C	D	Group E	F	G	H	Totals	Priority
1.	5	–	–	–	4	2	–	–	11	
2.	3	–	–	–	–	–	–	–	3	
3.	–	–	–	–	–	–	–	1	1	
4.	9	7	–	6	–	5	–	4	31	4
5.	–	–	8	–	–	–	–	2	10	
6.	–	–	9	–	–	–	7	–	16	
7.	–	8	2	3	8	8	8	10	47	2
8.	–	–	4	–	–	–	6	–	10	
9.	–	–	–	–	–	–	5	–	5	
10.	2	2	–	7	5	7	–	5	28	6
11.	8	10	7	8	–	9	10	6	58	1
12.	–	–	–	4	–	–	–	–	4	
13.	1	6	–	9	1	10	–	3	30	5
14.	–	1	–	1	10	–	2	9	23	8=
15.	–	–	–	–	–	–	–	–	9	
16.	–	–	3	–	3	4	–	–	14	
17.	7	–	10	–	6	–	–	–	23	8=
18.	10	9	–	–	7	–	9	7	42	3
19.	–	–	–	–	–	–	–	–	–	
20.	–	3	6	–	–	–	–	–	15	
21.	4	5	–	–	–	1	4	–	14	
22.	–	–	–	–	2	–	1	–	3	
23.	6	4	1	2	9	3	–	–	25	7
24.	–	–	–	5	–	–	–	–	5	
25.	–	–	–	10	–	–	3	8	21	10
26.	–	–	5	–	–	6	–	–	16	

So, the priorities agreed by the conference were:

1. become less paternalistic, more empowering in style (item 11, 58 points)
2. become more of a development agency, offering expertise as well as money (item 7, 47 points)
3. share resources and campaigns with other agencies like ourselves (item 18, 42 points)
4. put more effort into sponsoring fair trade—both overseas and in the UK (item 4, 31 points)
5. cut down on the number of projects and focus priorities more (item 13, 30 points)
6. recruit more young people (item 10, 28 points)
7. base new projects on better research and evaluation evidence (item 23, 25 pts)
8= concentrate on education about the developing world in the UK (item 14, 23 points)

8= recruit more black and Asian volunteers (item 17, 23 points)
10. ensure that all offices and premises have good access for the disabled (item 25, 21 points)

These priorities formed a major input into the Society's policy discussions for the next three-year plan.

In this example, it is interesting to note that many of the issues concerning this charitable organization have parallels in other sectors. Mergers, partnerships and staff involvement concern many large commercial businesses; and how to provide more for less is the preoccupation of many public services. Voluntary-sector 'companies', while part of the same species, live in only a partially different world.

The shadow side?   A further pressure on voluntary organizations is being felt from 'below'. Some user groups, in mental health for example, are finding their feet and voice and asserting their independence from even the voluntary agencies. In some areas, there is a trend towards the 'personalization' of voluntary activity, where local groups go it alone via community and church links, sending truckloads of medical supplies and sponsoring schools in Africa. Part of this is a reaction to the bigness and remoteness of some voluntary organizations, and also to what is seen as a paternalistic attitude on the part of the professional staff of that organization. Here is a strong example of the latter charge:

> The final paragraph of Nick Davies' article (September 1) describing how Nomad was effectively taken away from the people of Pye Bank by 'caring professionals' revealed the problem at the heart of much of the voluntary sector.
>
> Obtaining and hanging on to funding for social welfare is increasingly becoming the ends, rather than means, for too many voluntary organizations, leading to that paternalistic attitude which sees those in desperate need as 'clients' rather than people with hopes and aspirations. Unfortunately, 'knowing what's best' for the poor not only fails, to use the appropriate buzzword, to 'empower' working-class communities to organize for themselves, but also acts as a deadening hand that holds back attempts to deal with the causes of poverty.
>
> This situation is unlikely to get any better, particularly with the introduction of community care legislation which allows Social Services departments, rather than local people, to decide levels of service provision and contract out to compliant voluntary groups ....
>
> Middle-class social workers and the 'professionally concerned'

may, if they read this, splutter into their organically-grown coffee and protest that, at least, 'something is being done'. However, the reality is that institutionalized welfare services which bear little relation to the lives of those they claim to help are worse than useless. Unfortunately passing on the skills and experiences to make working-class self-organization possible does little to provide employment for the 'socially aware'. It is about time some groups and individuals asked themselves who it is they are really trying to help.

(Cuchulain, 1994)

Such a view again raises the old charge that voluntary work is a middle-class 'do-gooder' activity. Although the Volunteer Centre UK survey of 1991 did show that most of it was done by the middle-aged and well off, it also showed that 1 in 3 people with incomes of less that £4000 per annum made a contribution, as did 55 per cent of the 18 to 24s.

Voluntary organizations, like others in the public services, are faced daily with such demands. They are squeezed from above and from below. If they move too much towards becoming more professional service providers, this takes them away from that heartfelt and articulate user voice. And the users' views of what they want are almost inevitably different from the professionals' views of what is the appropriate service.

Can voluntary organizations become both more managerially and organizationally mature in order to secure the funding that ensures that at least 'something is done' while, at the same time, becoming more responsive to users?

Is it too much to hope that local authorities and other purchasers of services will become more creative in their contracting, sacrificing 'coverage' and uniformity for a diversity of provision, rewarding innovation, flexibility and closeness to the user?

Such an approach would support *small* learning companies in the voluntary sector, rather than the big, increasingly professional agencies of the State.

References

Batsleer, J. and Paton, R. (1993) 'Managing Voluntary Organizations in the Contract culture: Continuity or change', paper given to conference 'Contracting—Selling or Shrinking', South Bank University, London

Cuchulain, S. (1994) letter to *The Guardian*, 4 September

Drucker, P. (1990) *Managing the Non-profit Organization: Principles and practice*, HarperCollinsPublishers, New York

Gibran, K. (1926) *The Prophet*, Heinemann, Suffolk

Hinton, N. (1988) Foreword in Handy, C. *Understanding Voluntary Organizations*, Penguin, Harmondsworth, Middlesex

Handy, C. (1988) *Understanding Voluntary Organizations*, Penguin, Harmondsworth, Middlesex

Hayes, S. (1991) *Excursions into Learning in the Voluntary Sector*, MSc dissertation, Manchester Metropolitan University

Hunt, F. C. (1991) *Mastering Change Through Personal Transition*, MSc dissertation, Manchester Metropolitan University

Jarman, M. (1994) 'Together Towards 2000: A perspective from the voluntary sector', paper given to a NCVCCO/ADSS conference, Haydock

8   Good company

Whether we do well, whether we like ourselves, whether we lead
happy and productive lives, depends to a large extent on the
companies we choose. As the Greeks used to say, 'to live the
good life one must live in a great city'.
... In business ethics the corporation becomes one's immediate
community and, for better or for worse, the institution that
defines the values within which one lives much of one's life. A
corporation that encourages mutual cooperation and encourages
individual excellence as an essential part of teamwork is a very
different place to work and live than a corporation that incites
'either/or' competition, antagonism and continuous jostling for
status and recognition.
... The first principle of business ethics is that the corporation
is itself a citizen, a member of the larger community, and
inconceivable without it.

(Solomon, 1993, p. 148)

What is learning for? In the belief that all companies, public
and private, big and small, commercial and voluntary, are
members of the same species, this book looks at examples and
lessons of learning in different organizations, with a view to
understanding them, making them known and encouraging
their transfer. We discover that, whatever the kind of
organization, when learning is a central preoccupation, questions of value lie immediately behind. What *is* learning for?

All meaningful knowledge is for the sake of action, and all
meaningful action for the sake of friendship.

(J. Macmurray, in Revans, 1983, p. 6)

If we would bring about the learning company, can we
assume that this is also a *good company*?

When Peters and Waterman produced a list of 'excellent'
companies in their book *In Search of Excellence* (Harper and Row,
1982), they were criticized among other things for using financial
performance or profit as the sole criterion of 'excellence'. By this

definition, it doesn't count if a company pays low wages and provides poor working conditions for employees; it doesn't matter whether its operations damage the environment or that it uses its buying power to force its suppliers' prices down in poor countries. In fact, on financial performance alone, doing these things would make an even more 'excellent' company.

(Pedler, Burgoyne and Boydell, 1991, p. 76)

As a 'naïve' secretary working in a business school, Coralie Palmer describes her shock at the self-absorption, the disregard for the unpleasant consequences of actions and the jargon used to circumvent the truth that she found in the business community. She sees this behaviour as fundamentally adolescent:

> If you look up that word [equity] in the *Oxford English Dictionary* you will find two, seemingly unrelated, kinds of meaning. The first concerns 'stocks and shares not bearing fixed interest; or the value of shares issued by a company'. This is the set of meanings with which businesses are comfortably familiar. But the second definition describes Equity as 'fairness; recourse to principles of justice to correct or supplement law ...'. It's this sense of the word 'Equity' that needs to be restored to the business world if it is going to be able to move from spotty adolescence to responsible adulthood.
>
> (1994, p. 61)

And adolescent behaviour can slip into criminality:

> Union Carbide's response to Bhopal was, in the opinion of many critics, unethical and inhumane, but it was not illegal. However data from various researchers show that two-thirds of the *Fortune 500* companies *have* been involved in illegal behaviour between 1975 and 1985. *US News and World Report* states that 115 of the 500 were convicted of a serious crime during the 1980s.
>
> (Hawken, 1993, p. 116)

Are all companies learning companies?

Yes. Any company that continues to exist must be fulfilling some purpose and have learned, at least at the simple level of remembering, what works and be able to repeat it. The current interest in learning organizations stems from the fact that this rudimentary type of learning is no longer adequate for most companies. Just continuing with what worked in the past, without innovating, developing and improving is likely to lead to failure—either by rejection from users with changing needs or by the market, as consumers move to more innovative firms.

Burgoyne suggests that there are 'weak' and 'strong' forms of the learning company:

> At the first level the organization has a kind of memory. It learns processes, then puts them into procedures and keeps them going. Here is the classic phenomenon of bureaucracy.
>
> ... The second level is of organizations that can be described as adapting systems ... Such organizations manage to change and adapt to meet the changing demands of markets, economies, social interest or political systems which determine their survival. These are primarily self-interested organizations and the outcome of their learning is their survival. In the commercial sphere, it is this level of performance that is largely rewarded within free market, capitalist systems .... Second level learning organizations will tend to exploit their customers, clients, employees, suppliers, neighbours, raw materials and even owners. They will erect their own needs as they exhaust the old ones and move on to new territory.
>
> Third level learning organizations develop their contexts, make their own world better for them to live in and to contribute to ... will act in a way that assists the development and enrichments of the organization's stakeholders, resources, trading partners ...
>
> (1992, p. 323)

Similarly, Harrison and Spoth refer to '... three levels of organization consciousness: Transactional, Self-expression, Mutuality', as measured by their 'Organization Culture Scan' (1992).

The companies dubbed 'excellent' by Peters and Waterman locate at level 2 in this typology; and this is still, a decade and a half on, the dominant 'role model' for companies, especially, but by no means exclusively, in the commercial sector. At level 2, the 'excellent company' defines the 'good company'. The ecological level 3 steps beyond this, recognizing an interconnected world in which each company's actions enrich or impoverish the whole, echoing Bateson's view that 'The unit of survival is a flexible organism-in-its-environment':

> It is now empirically clear that Darwinian evolutionary theory contained a very real error in its identification of the unit of survival under natural selection. The unit which was believed to be crucial and around which the theory was set up was either the breeding individual or the family line or subspecies or some similar homogeneous set of conspecifics. Now I suggest that the last hundred years have demonstrated empirically that if an organism or aggregate of organisms sets to work with a focus on its own survival and thinks that this is the way to select its adaptive moves, its 'progress' ends up with a destroyed environ-

ment. If the organism ends up by destroying its environment, it has in fact destroyed itself ... The unit of survival is a flexible organism-in-its-environment.

(1968, p. 425 and 426)

The need to move beyond level 2 is signalled by Kanter (1994), who suggests that today 'collaborative advantage' must replace or at least augment the competitive advantage ethic of the 1980s. But does 'collaborative advantage' truly go beyond the individual success/survival of level 2 or has the 'individual' just got bigger, becoming, through alliances, part of a cartel or a consortium? Have we really changed our view of 'the unit of survival'?

If we want learning organizations, we must also get better at identifying and mitigating any adverse effects of our actions and learning. Try the test in Application 15 on your company.

Application 15: Learning and its consequences

We tend to take it for granted that learning and development are good things in themselves. Our very definition of the word 'development' implies some movement to a more advanced or improved state where the person or the team or the company is more knowledgeable, more able, more effective.

But is learning automatically a good thing? The saying *'A little learning is a dangerous thing'* attests both to the power of knowledge and to its possible unintended consequences. Perhaps we can think of personal examples when we would rather not have known something or where we have used a new skill—a new strength—carelessly. Can you think of examples where any of the companies you know have fallen into a similar trap?

Of course, many of the consequences of learning are good; we learn new things all the time to improve things. However, curious and anxious to learn as we are, there is usually an unintended aspect.

Here is a simple activity for thinking through the possible consequences of some learning or development in which your company is currently involved.

1. Think of something your company is currently learning about—some trial, pilot study, experiment or development; the testing of a new type of product or service, perhaps, or venturing into a new type of work or market, an organizational change or a new collaboration or partnership. What's new at the moment? Where is the learning edge in your company?

2. When you have chosen a 'learning edge', write down all the things the company intends to achieve or gain through this development. Use your imagination to think of all the possible benefits.

1 _____

2 _____

3 _____

4 _____

5 _____

6 _____

3. Now, try to imagine the worst—what could be the bad, unintended—consequences of this development or learning? Be Cassandra for a moment—she who warned the Trojans that their curiosity about the Greeks' wooden horse would come to no good, but was not believed. Are there any 'wooden horse' implications of this new learning for:

• the company as a whole?

_____

_____

• any individuals in the company?

_____

_____

• suppliers of the company?

_____

_____

• customers or users?

_____

_____

• the local community or environment?

_____

_____

- anyone else?

  _____

  _____

4. Now, cast off your prophet's garb and become yourself an enlightened Trojan. What could be done *now* to mitigate some of these possibly disastrous consequences. Learning and development tend to have a momentum of their own, but we can sometimes make a difference if we foresee certain outcomes and seek to guard against them. In terms of the possible effects of the learning in which your company is currently engaged, what could be done for:

- the company as a whole?

  _____

  _____

  _____

- any individuals in the company?

  _____

  _____

  _____

- suppliers of the company?

  _____

  _____

  _____

- customers or users?

  _____

  _____

  _____

- for the local community or environment?

  _____

  _____

  _____

- anyone else?

_____

_____

_____

5. If you've got this far, well done. Now, make an action plan. Good luck.

The best companies do try to guard against the shadow side of learning and development by exercising this sort of 'moral imagination'. This is a good thing because they tend to be better at learning and are therefore more likely to be in danger of such unintended consequences. It is possible to foresee that technological developments are likely to make some jobs redundant and take steps to re-train or protect those likely to be affected. A good company making business decisions that might have unpleasant impacts on a local community or environment could institute an inquiry or learning process to see how these effects could be mitigated, where a bad company might be secretive, try to bypass planning procedures or otherwise work against these wider interests.

At level 3, the good company is trying to think beyond the immediate and make a wider contribution—like Tom's of Maine.

CASE: Tom's of Maine

Tom Chappell of Tom's of Maine (the New England toothpaste and personal health products manufacturer) decided, as the small family business grew, not to go and do an MBA but to attend divinity school instead. The subtitle of Tom Chappell's book—*Managing for Profit and the Common Good*—confirms the idea of balance (1993). Tom's of Maine, founded by Tom and Kate Chappell in 1970, was the first company to market a toothpaste made entirely from natural ingredients. By 1981, the company's turnover reached $1.5 million and, five years later, $5 million, but Tom was not happy:

> I owned a six-bedroom, eighteenth-century Federal-style house on Main Street in a picture-postcard New England town. I had two cars and a forty-foot Hinckley sailing yawl. I had five terrific kids, three of them in boarding school. The woman I loved and respected was not only my wife but my business partner. I had achieved, it seemed, the American dream and then some. But ... I felt something was missing, something was wrong. I was miserable.
>
> (1993, p. xi)

In 1986, at the age of 43, and after 'discussions with wise friends', Tom Chappell went to the Harvard Divinity School, where he was strongly influenced by the philosophies of Martin Buber and New England's own Jonathon Edwards. A century before Buber's 'I and Thou', Edwards wrote that 'one alone is nothing' and that identity comes not from our separation but our connectedness with others:

> I now found myself thinking about Tom's of Maine in light of Jonathon Edwards, about my company not only as a private entity but in relation to many other entities—employees, financial partners, customers, suppliers, even the earth itself. Living in a community, we are relational, and we have obligations that go along with those relationships .... In those relationships I began to see the basis for a new approach to a business plan.
>
> (1993, pp. 16–18)

There were doubters on the Board, who could see the new plan leading to greater social responsibility but who feared for the profits. In 1992, turnover increased by 31 per cent, profit by 40 per cent—up from the hardly pedestrian 25 per cent average of the previous five years. Tom's of Maine gives 10 per cent of its pre-tax profits to worthy causes and employees get childcare subsidies and time off for voluntary work in the community. It also produces innovative, healthy products. On each toothpaste packet it says:

> Dear Customers and Old Friends,
> For over 20 years we have committed ourselves to natural additive-free body care products. From the early days we have created products with natural ingredients that work as well as or better than commercial brands without using preservatives, artifical dyes, synthetic sweeteners and flavors, or animal by-products. Our company has grown but our approach remains simple and direct. We listen to what you want (and don't want) in your products; we learn how it can be done, and we respond with intelligent alternatives.
>
> Putting into words our mission as a company has helped us affirm our beliefs and identify new ways to serve you. Part of our mission at Tom's of Maine is 'to be distinctive in products and policies which honor and sustain our natural world'. That is why our ingredients are biodegradable, our toothpaste cartons are made of recycled board (95 per cent post-consumer waste), our tubes are recyclable, and we don't test on animals.
> Thank you for using our products and let us know what you think.

Tom Chappell's aims now encompass changing the wider business culture to one in which private profit and the common good can work together. He believes that this is beginning to happen and, as the $20 million business heads towards becoming a $100 million one, he says:

> I began as a selfish entrepreneur. Now I would like to become an entrepreneur committed to others. But I remain a competitor. I still love the game of business, the struggle, the winning. I used to think ... [I would go] into politics ... in the last few years I have realized that I can have a bigger impact on changing things as a successful businessman.
>
> (1993, p. 218)

The Good Company and the Nice Company

Tom Lloyd's 'nice companies' make good profits like Tom's of Maine, but there are some profound philosophical differences. The 'nice company's' strategy is:

> 'tit-for-tat' ... of never being the first to defect. A nice company is a cooperative company. It behaves as if it recognizes the intrinsic positive-sum nature of the business game. It is competitive in a general sense in that it wishes to win the tournament—to make the most profit—but it is predisposed to be cooperative in particular situations. I've proposed a law of business which states that the sum of the business game is maximized when cooperation is maximized.
>
> (1990, pp. 220 and 221)

Lloyd's definition of 'nice companies' is based on the biological model of Dawkins' 'selfish gene' and holds that companies only negotiate long term with those who follow collaborative rather than adversarial strategies. 'Niceness' can thus embrace Amstrad, Hewlett-Packard, Pearson and Virgin as well the ecologically sound The Body Shop—all being 'value added partnerships'. Here we are back to collaborative advantage and, indeed, to 'excellence'; Lloyd's 'nice companies' are up-to-date versions of Peters and Waterman's excellent ones—with added partnership!

Tom's of Maine sounds nice, too, but very different. Here, a conventional, well-established business, turns to spiritual and ethical guidance rather than business management advice to lift its purpose and still succeeds commercially—in fact, even more so. This is closer to The Body Shop's 'ethical business is good business' perspective.

The nice company ⟵ Tom's of Maine ⟶ The good company

Our next company, Traidcraft, aims to be a successful business because this is the best way of putting over the message of fair trade, that it is possible as well as desirable to do fair, equitable business. Different again from Tom's of Maine or The Body Shop, ethics *is* Traidcraft's business.

CASE: Traidcraft plc

Traidcraft plc was founded as a trading company in 1979 and now works with over 100 overseas suppliers from 26 countries in Asia, Africa and Latin America. It employs some 150 people at its head office and warehouse in Gateshead, selling imported handicrafts, clothing, books, cards and paper products, tea and coffee through a network of some 2000 volunteer representatives and retailers. By March 1994, sales turnover had reached £6.6 million (up 13 per cent on the year), profit after tax was £51 000, and the Board declared a nil dividend to shareholders.

Like other companies, Traidcraft has a distinctive set of values that guides its day-to-day business activities. In a tradition that goes back to and beyond some of the great Victorian business founders, these values mix commercial and social objectives. Drawing on its Christian roots, Traidcraft's mission is 'trading for a fairer world' or, as the *Basis of Faith* (1989) puts it, 'the promotion of greater love and justice in the trading process'. Yet, Traidcraft plc is no charity—it trades to make a profit and it is as hard-headed about its business purposes as any other global company:

> Traidcraft is not a charity; we're a growing business enterprise. We are not just selling goods; we're challenging the way the rich exploit the poor. We are demonstrating that trade with developing countries can and should be based on justice, concern for people, partnership between rich and poor and care for the environment.'
>
> (Catalogue, 1989/90)

Traidcraft does have a charitable arm—Traidcraft Exchange. It has two purposes: to provide business support and development help for overseas producers and to do educational and awareness-raising work in the UK. As part of the Fair Trade Foundation with its pioneering 'Fair Trade Mark' logo, much of Traidcraft's campaigning and educational purpose is done in collaboration with other organizations. One such collaboration, Cafédirect Limited, has managed to get fairly traded coffee onto the shelves of the big supermarket chains and is beginning to make an impact on the UK's £550 million coffee market.

As one manager explained, although working for a fairer trading system is Traidcraft's ultimate purpose, financial viability and profit are also critical business goals:

> If we increase sales 10-fold, 20-fold and not increase the profit on those sales, then we're not doing the producers justice ... and that is our ultimate goal. So, being as profitable as we can means that we can expand the business and the number of people we are dealing with .... Traidcraft is about giving an example that an organization can trade fairly and ethically and still make money. If you can do well and make a profit while still trading fairly and not exploiting people, that's a really good example for other businesses.

The company holds itself responsible for dealing fairly with producers, staff, consumers and the wider public, voluntary representatives and retailers, and shareholders—and all without damaging the environment.

Perfect plc?

Such high standards inevitably raise expectations. The continuous open and public demonstration of intent brings some interesting tensions into Traidcraft. As a director pointed out, one of the problems is that people have very high expectations of the management and of the organization, and 'We invariably fall short of these'. Another commented:

> Most people are here not just because it's a job, but because they want to be

here ... they care far more about their work than they would elsewhere and they want the best from the organization. There's a sense of self-criticism and frustration in pushing themselves quite hard. What happens in Traidcaft is that there is this notional 'perfect plc' ... we always compare ourselves with that and everyone has their own individual 'perfect plc'.

These habits of openness and self-criticism put the company well beyond the recommendations of the Cadbury Report (Cadbury, 1992). This 'code of best practice' suggests guidelines for good corporate governance, especially concerning matters of reporting and the appointment of non-executive directors to oversee important aspects of company affairs. Although some large UK companies show no signs of implementing this advice, Cadbury's code looks very 'weak' to one Traidcraft manager:

When we looked at Cadbury and heard a lot of listed companies say 'How are we going to cope with that?' we said, 'Oh, is that all!' ... it's fairly easy for us to be quite open about what the risks are to the business and talking about the future, whereas, I understand some companies will be having difficulty with that because their reports have been more PR documents, dodging the issues and hiding mistakes.

Traidcraft as a learning company

Traidcraft's habits of self-reflection and openness are particular strengths that have an important impact on how people learn in the company. One of the directors made a strong link between values in Traidcraft and these learning habits:

A precondition for learning in Traidcraft that might be unusual comes from Christian values ... you can go wrong, you can make mistakes ... [this] can inform some of the processes in the workplace where there's a degree of tolerance, and a degree of forgiveness and a degree of optimism about the results of facing up to failure that's not common, I think, in normal business practice. The practice of repentance and forgiveness and renewal is a daily experience.

In Traidcraft, it is common to find people emphasizing the importance of learning and of being a learning organization. One person said that, at Traidcraft, the learning company is about seeing change as creating flexibility in the organization—'that's something I think we're trying to learn to live with more ... instead of seeing change as 'let's get this done and then get back to work' ... seeing it as more or less continuous'. A manager contrasted the company's attitude to innovation with her previous working environment:

I worked in a bank with lots of standard operating procedures ... you could innovate but it was hard work! I was a bolshie sod when I worked there so I did try to change things. The big difference here is that people who would not naturally innovate are encouraged to do so.

Social accounting

Traidcraft's key vehicle for learning as a company is the Social Accounting Report. Part of the company's 'ambitious strategic intent', this is an annual account by Traidcraft plc of the social, economic and ethical effects of its business activities. The 1993/4 Social Accounting Report examines the perspectives of key stakeholders, including producers or suppliers (because of costs, a sample of producer groups are surveyed each year); staff or employees; voluntary representatives and retailers; the wider public and environmental issues. Shareholders were surveyed in the 1992/3 report and consumers are included in the plan for the next report.

Social accounting runs alongside and incorporates other search processes. For example, in 1994, Tyneside Training and Enterprise Council conducted an analysis for the Investors in People Award and an independent consultant carried out a company audit of 'corporate spirituality' (Conn 1994). The social accounting process, now in its third year, is still developing and is making a significant contribution to learning in the company.

Accounting for the social, economic and ethical impact of Traidcraft's business activities, social accounting is a good example of an effort of corporate responsibility. In acknowledging this, it is important also to recognize its strategic value to the company. Through consulting with all the groups of people involved in or affected by Traidcraft's activities, the social accounting process creates policy and direction, and helps shape the future business:

> The social accounting process recognizes that the Traidcraft dynamic is not about a few good and great trying to work out what it means to do fair trade, but it is about listening to the people who are the Fair Trade movement and finding ways of hearing their expectations and reflections of what Traidcraft is doing and balancing that with our inherited quality framework and the inherited values, and the foundation principles'.

... and is central to its learning processes:

> We've made an investment in time and resources into something which is helping us corporately learn about Traidcraft. Without the Social Accounting Report we'd read our glossy annual report—we'd read it, we'd love it, we'd get on with our work. What's happening now is that, through the year, we're quoting the Report to ourselves, we're talking about what shareholders said about us, what producer partners said. I've only seen a snippet of what's being done this year and already it's bringing out huge questions ... not only in tangible things, such as developing non-financial performance indicators, but also our day-to-day activities, it's coming up all the time and is very closely linked to our corporate learning.

The effects of the social accounting process can be traced throughout the 11 characteristics of the learning company (Pedler, Burgoyne and Boydell, 1991, pp. 18–20). It has a particularly significant part to play in developing 'strategy as a learning process', 'participative policy making' and in 'formative accounting'. Central to the process is the valuing of 'boundary workers as environmental scanners', as the antennae of the company. These aspects are especially important in those companies—including public services, voluntary organizations and ethically driven companies—where the simple measure of profit is not enough to reconcile all the dilemmas. The social accounting process is part of creating a 'learning climate' within Traidcraft. It is designed to be:

> ... an educative tool with a distinctive perspective from the intention of most financial audits ... it would be a positive outcome for stakeholders to be encouraged to engage in the process of resolving complex ethical issues that have no crude objective means of resolution
>
> (Zadek and Evans, 1993, p. 29)

External Affairs Director Richard Evans rejects the idea that such an audit is only appropriate for 'ethical' organizations, commenting that 'in the real world, the reverse is true' (Evans, 1993, p. 4). In conducting their analysis for the Investors in People Award, the Tyneside Training and Enterprise Council would seem to agree:

> The Christian faith sits comfortably with the criteria of Investors in People and contemporary thinking on how employees should be supported and managed.

Zadek and Evans (1993, pp. 31 and 32) summarize the distinctive features of Traidcraft's social accounting as:

Stakeholder perspective the key role played by stakeholders in defining what performance indicators are to be used, as well as providing views and other information to enable performance to be measured against these indicators.

Comparative the report should offer means of comparing with the organization's objectives and those of key stakeholders, with its performance over time and in relation to other organizations where this is relevant and possible.

Comprehensive it should, over time, attempt to reflect the impact of all the company's activities on stakeholder groups and the environment, whether this be through total coverage of such activities or sampling.

Polyvocal it should be based on, and record the views and accounts of, stakeholders themselves, as well as those of the company and the auditors. Thus the audit does not offer a 'universal' or singular voice, but, rather, is in itself a *social* document.

Spiritual the methodology must be open to recognizing the role spiritual values play in stakeholders' perceptions and aspirations, and in the management of the life of the organization.

Learning our understanding is that the social audit is an essential tool in a learning organization and that its comprehensiveness extends to the potential to increase learning capacity it extends to all stakeholders.

Regular social audits should take place annually, although not all aspects may be covered every year for cost reasons.

Externally validated by independent auditors, who must decide whether the report offers a 'fair and reasonable' picture of the organization's social impact and ethical behaviour against its objectives and those of its stakeholder groups.

Disclosure the social audit should be made available to all stakeholders, preferably with the statutory financial statements, and in advance of the Annual General Meeting, to which other stakeholders, as well as shareholders, should be invited.

Nearly perfect plc?

In many ways, Traidcraft is just like any other good business organization. After concerns were voiced about its management style, it has set out to move away from a 'command' model to a more participative, teamwork-based style. Traidcraft wants to be as innovative in its organization as in its trading policies. As one manager commented, Traidcraft is:

> ... a very businesslike organization ... it aspires to be very professional at a high level, profit is not the motivator but it's not a cranky organization. It's an innovative organization striving to be very business-like and some of the things which may have been quite weird a few years ago are actually the norm outside. The things we're highlighting in our work, things like a horizontal organization, are quite new thinking. Traidcraft wants to be at the edge of business thought as well everything else.

Traidcraft has some unique business advantages—its unpaid sales force, its highly committed staff and its altruistic shareholders. These must be weighed against the ambition of its aims. Traidcraft aims to set a good example, but it also has its, almost impossibly high, expectations and the many tensions and continuous questioning these bring.

As in other companies, one of the tensions is the balancing of the returns to the various stakeholders. These can often be in conflict as, for example, where higher dividend payments to shareholders might be balanced by higher prices for customers. Traidcraft has unusual shareholders who do not expect a financial return. Perhaps because of this altruism, these investors of almost £2 million in Traidcraft have tended to come at the end of the queue of stakeholders. In recent years, and especially through its social accounting process, Traidcraft has set out to be more responsive to the interests of investors.

Tyneside Training and Enterprise Council's summing up of Traidcraft is balanced:

> In Traidcraft, the team found a strong commitment to corporate success from management and the workforce in general .... The management in Traidcraft must take credit for the way employees understand and subscribe to the core business of the company .... In particular the open management style, the excellent communications systems and the teambuilding activities have done a great deal to bring about the commitment referred to. Managers are visible, readily accessible, and take a genuine interest in the well-being of their staff ...
>
> Normally at this stage a review of the barriers to implementing Investors in People takes place. In the case of Traidcraft, many of the barriers normally perceived are down .... The main issues appear to be around tightening up or reaffirming understanding of what is required by all parties. In particular manager responsibilities and the setting of standards for training and development need work. Evaluating the whole of the activity would also benefit from strategic planning.
>
> (Tyneside Training and Enterprise Council, 1994, p. 10)

No matter how far you've come, when you set yourself ambitions like Traidcraft, there is always plenty left to do for the learning organization.

Ethical trading

It might be thought that Traidcraft is peculiar or unique and, therefore, not much of an example to 'mainstream' businesses. Of course, Traidcraft does have unique aspects, and there are few businesses with shareholders committed enough to forego financial dividends and see their capital actually decline through inflation! But, all businesses have unique aspects, business advantages that are not reproduced elsewhere. It is argued, for example that companies in Japan are fortunate in having shareholders and bankers less insistent on short-term dividends and more committed to long-term success than those in the West, but this does not stop us trying to learn from them.

There are an increasing number of businesses seeking to trade ethically. In the USA, there are now 700 members of Business for Social Responsibility, an umbrella group that includes many small companies similar to Traidcraft as well as giants such as Levi Strauss. Attempting to trade ethically creates new problems and dilemmas. To do it you must be ready for these to be the vehicles for an organizational learning process that will, eventually, perhaps, transform the business. For example:

> Stride Rite, a Boston shoemaker with a finely honed social conscience, has won 14 public service awards in the past 3 years, including one for 'improving the quality of life' in its community and the nation. But that has not prevented it closing down its plant in Boston and moving production to Kentucky, where labour costs are lower—although turnover has doubled to more than $600 million [£400 million] in the past eight years.
>
> (Elliot, 1994)

Even nice guys have to be competitive. Good companies, like good people, are not unmixed. The Stride Rite case illustrates how aiming at 'ethical business' will always raise high expectations and lay you open to criticism. The UK's The Body Shop made this painful discovery in 1994, but managed to ride the storm and recover its share price. Can we learn to cope with both a high aspiration and a mixed experience of behaviour that invariably falls short from time to time?

Unmixed purity would be hard to take anyway, not only in the business world, but this is not really the purpose or the point. If we erect the aspiration to be good and define what we mean by that, then this inevitably brings us to face the darker side of ourselves. If we set out to run a good business, this aim requires us, like Traidcraft and the others mentioned here, to examine carefully all aspects of our behaviour to see how well we are doing. And there is always a down side, a dark side that reflects our strengths in strange and unpleasant ways. Coming to terms with the dark side of a person or a company is a critical act of self- or organizational development.

Significant learning—that which changes a person or an organization—is always concerned with moral values, of right and wrong, or right living and working. If we are going to get better at learning, then we must also increase our capacity for making moral judgements in order to set ourselves and others higher, not lower, standards.

Ethical trading means moving towards Morris' view of the 'good company' by seeking to balance the interests of all stakeholders (Morris, 1987). This is a learning adventure indeed, as Tom's of Maine found out, and it is one that more and more companies are seeking. One way of moving this way is to take a 'balanced scorecard' approach to accounting and reporting (Kaplan and Norton, 1992 and 1993).

The balanced scorecard

The notion of the 'balanced scorecard' implies that perform-ance measures based solely on returns to the providers of financial capital are unbalanced. Kaplan and Norton propose measures of customer satisfaction, internal operations and organizational learning and innovation, as well as financial performance. This has been developed in Skandia, a multi-national financial services company, by Leif Edvisson, in a way that shows that the very notion of capital can be broadened (Brownfield, 1994). This is shown in Figure 8.1.

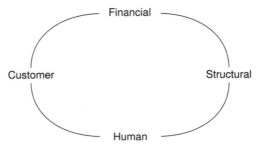

Figure 8.1   Capital in the Balanced Scorecard

The notion of *financial* capital is mainly well understood, although there are difficult issues, such as that of 'intellectual capital'. *Human* capital is the knowledge, skills and experi-ence of people—what they need to know to create the product or service, develop the business, maximize their contributions and so on. *Structural* capital is the extension of human capital through tools and enabling systems, for example, organizational manuals and procedures, databases, information technology systems and networks. *Customer* capital is the positive regard and continuing support of users and consumers. Other types of capital—of trading partners, suppliers, the local community and so on—can also be included. However, the main point is that of devising appropriate measures in these areas that will enable comparisons and balancings to be made.

Once you have defined the categories of 'capital' you consider to be important, it then takes some ingenuity to come up with appropriate measures. Skandia has a fast-growing Assurance and Financial Services Division (AFS), with a Director and a Comptroller of Intellectual Capital. Measures of *financial* capital (net asset values development) and *customer* capital (number of accounts, surrender and turnover ratios) are fairly obvious, but *human* capital includes the number of female leaders as well as the more usual costs of training per employee and turnover. AFS measures 'knowledge networking' as well as 'money networking' and reports measures of intellectual capital in its annual report (Brownfield, 1994).

The Development and Learning Function (D&L) of the Digital Equipment Corporation is another instructive example. Against Digital's recent history of losses, massive change, 'downsizing' and restructuring, the D&L is charged with 'increasing workforce and organizational capability to meet customer demands'. Some of the measures that the D&L has proposed to assess progress on regarding this aim are:

- *financial* 'percentage of all learning solutions with learning objectives which clearly relate to business results'
- *customer* 'the number of learning solutions which support customer goals'
- *human* 'the number of internal departments in Digital which have formal capability assessment processes for their people'
- *structural* 'requests v offers'—a way of measuring the D&L's readiness to respond—and 'best practices implemented'—a way of testing the effectiveness of learning solutions.

The meaning of some of these measures does not translate easily outside the environment of the particular company in which they are developed and make sense, but the direction of the thinking is clear and the effort to measure value added, particularly to human and intellectual capital, is intriguing.

What we can begin to measure we can begin to control—or at least understand.

One final example from Digital's D&L is their attempt to measure the idea of 'knowledge turn', based on the metaphor of inventory turnover, and defined as 'best practices institutionalized'. There are several stages to the knowledge turn:

- identifying a potential best practice
- disseminating it
- getting others to adopt/adapt/implement it
- turning it into standard operating practice and franchising it. (Brownfield, 1994).

A 'knowledge turn' is a way of measuring the rate at which an organization is able to learn, apply and share new knowledge. There are encouraging precedents for this—medical education in the UK is traditionally based on an apprentice system for doctors that has been (slightly) satirized as 'see one, do one, teach one'—and the work of creating indicators of organizational learning is a critical area for research and development. While still in its early stages, the last part of this chapter offers an approach to developing these indicators for your company.

Developing performance indicators

How can we develop such tests to help us measure the success or otherwise of our efforts? The term 'performance indicator' (PI) has many synonyms, such as 'critical success factor' or the simpler 'success criteria', which all attest to a desire to measure things that have been hitherto intangible and hard to quantify. You may well have a term of your own that is 'a statement against which achievement in an area or activity can be assessed'. Performance indicators are:

> ... useful for setting goals and clarifying objectives. For some performance indicators, a brief statement is sufficient; for others the statement should be more specific and refer to supplementary processes which would give a measure of depth, quality and/or commitment in a particular area.
>
> (Hopkins and Leask, 1989, pp. 6–7)

PIs are part of evaluation processes in all types of organizations. They are, of course, not without problems. Not least, hard work is often necessary to create good ones, especially in those areas of your operations where simple, quantifiable measures are unavailable. However, the very process of creating PIs is a valuable one from which those who get involved can learn a great deal about the purpose of the business and its effects. Application 16 offers a process you can follow or adopt to your own purposes.

Application 16: Creating performance indicators

This process begins by looking at how you measure performance in your company at present. These measures may be explicit or implicit, quantified or not. Whichever they are, start by writing them down.

Step 1 Can you list the indicators currently used to measure performance in your company:

by yourself?

_____

_____

_____

_____

_____

by your immediate colleagues?

_____

_____

_____

_____

_____

more widely in your organization?

_____

_____

_____

_____

_____

by your key stakeholders?

_____

_____

_____

_____

_____

Step 2 How many areas of performance await the development of indicators 'when there is the time'?

_____

_____

_____

_____

_____

Which aspects of your work are proving most difficult to measure?

_____

_____

_____

_____

_____

Are aspects of your work being crowded out or devalued by the parts that are more easily measurable?

_____

_____

_____

_____

_____

These questions are often difficult to answer. Although some PIs look simple, especially when imposed from outside, you can't go through the process of setting indicators without engaging in some serious debate. For example, we can't ask, 'How are we doing?' if we are unclear about what we're trying to achieve or against which standards we are holding ourselves.

Step 3 Specifying PIs. A systematic process for developing PIs (Aspinwall, _et al._, 1992, Ch. 6) suggests that the first task is to identify the key _performance areas_; then to identify _success criteria_ for each area; determine the _kinds of data_ that need to be collected and analysed: determine the basis for _comparison_; and consider any _particular circumstances_ that may need to be taken into account in judging performance, thus:

Performance area	
Success criteria	
Data collection	
Comparator/s	
Contextual factors	

First, identify an area of performance for which you need to develop some indicators of success. To complete the rest of this chart work through the following questions.

(i) What are we trying to achieve?

_____

_____

_____

_____

_____

(The most critical question, sometimes requiring considerable thought and discussion to identify the key dimensions of achievement. Only when this is done can you move on to a consideration of specific indicators of success.)

(ii) What would be appropriate indicators of success?

_____

_____

_____

_____

_____

(It is important to develop a systematic framework for all major performance areas so that suitable indicators can be developed for each.)

(iii)   How should data be gathered and processed?

_____

_____

_____

_____

_____

(Quantitative or qualitative data or both? Can you ensure that the resources—usually time and skill—needed to process the data will be available?)

(iv)   Against what can you validate the results?

_____

_____

_____

_____

_____

(Any evidence of performance must be comparative. 'We're doing OK' or 'We could do better' both imply (unstated) standards. The most common types of standard for making judgements about achievements are:

- *comparative* how we compare with similar developments elsewhere
- *progress* how we are doing compared to the past
- *target* how we are doing against any standard or target(s) we have set ourselves or others have set for us

These probably require us to look inside and outside the organization.)

(v)   What other information is necessary to put the results into context?

_____

_____

_____

_____

_____

(Are we making valid comparisons? Is like being compared with like? However, beware of using this question for special pleading—to argue that your organization's situation is unique. There seem to be more cases of this being used to excuse poor performance than to explain good!)

Step 4 Making use of PIs. The next critical step is to establish the legitimacy of the information gathered. What conclusions can legitimately be drawn from this evidence?

Ask yourself

- *Is it relevant? Does it tell us what we need to know?* It is too easy to collect masses of easily available information or to collect far more than is necessary because it appears 'interesting'.
- *Is it adequate? Does it reflect the full range or complexity of an issue or just a limited view?* This is particularly likely to occur if only one stakeholder is involved in any discussions.
- *Is it valid? Does it represent what it is supposed to represent?* Quantified, and standardized, measures are much easier to deal with and may be the most convenient basis for external comparability. However, crucial areas of performance often need more qualitative measures.
- *Is it reliable? Would similar conclusions be reached if the information was obtained by somebody else or in some other way?* Again, this may be easier with quantitative rather than qualitative indicators and can emphasize those elements that are easier to measure and are less likely to provide depth of understanding. Collecting more than one kind of data by different methods helps with reliability.

Check the quality of any data collection exercise by recording its strengths and weaknesses in the following matrix.

Performance area: _____

	Strengths of information	Weaknesses of information
Relevance		
Adequacy		
Validity		
Reliability		

What will you be able to claim in the light of this analysis? If you claim things that your information can't support, this may damage the credibility of the whole exercise.

Step 5 Last but not least, what action do you intend to take?

_____

_____

_____

_____

_____

At the end of this process, you should be able to produce PIs that are straightforward and clear. Aim for a relatively small number that capture the key dimensions of success, while avoiding oversimplification. Make sure that you have involved key stakeholders (see Chapter 6) where and when appropriate. Everyone who needs to know should be clear about:

- what indicators are to be used
- why they were chosen
- what information is to be collected in relation to them
- how the outcomes of the process will be used.

Remember to keep asking 'What use is this information?'—the collection of data is not in itself a virtue. However, the intelligent use and interpretation of information about performance can be a powerful influence for change, development and learning.

A question of balance

For John Morris (1987) a 'good company' seeks 'mutual advantage', a subtly different line from the, perhaps necessary, virtue of collaborative advantage, by balancing the interests of all stakeholders. He is concerned to balance the enormous appeal of the 'excellence' ethic, with its lopsided leaning towards the interests of capital, with the warmth and strength of the good company of colleagues, allies and friends who support us in our everyday attempts to keep body and soul together—to 'just manage'. The managers' job is to meet the expectations of investors, customers, employees, managers (as a subgroup of employees), suppliers and the public, delivering a different sort of quality to each. For example:

- owners seek _quality of business performance_ and quality of management
- consumers want value for money and _quality of service_

- employees want *quality of working life*
- the public seeks an acceptable *quality of social responsibility.*

So, the 'good company' contributes to the needs of a widening group of stakeholders and looks beyond itself to the wider community, a theme we take further in Chapter 9.

References

Aspinwall, K., Simpkins, T., Wilkinson, J. and McAuley, J. (1992) *Managing Evaluation in Education*, Routledge, London

Bateson, G. (1968) *Steps to an Ecology of Mind*, Paladin, London

Brownfield, S. (1994) 'Quantum Measures: Indicators for learning organizations', USA Learning Company Conference Papers, Learning Company Project, Sheffield

Burgoyne, J. G. (April 1992) 'Creating a Learning Organization', *RSA Journal*, CXL (5428)

Cadbury, A. (1992) *Report of the Committee on the Financial Aspects of Corporate Governance*, Gee, London

Chappell, T. (1993) *The Soul of a Business: Managing for profit and the common good*, Bantam, New York

Conn, E. (April 1994) *Corporate Spirituality: A company audit*, unpublished report to Traidcraft plc

Elliot, L. (18 June 1994) 'Greenbacks love Green Business' *The Guardian*

Evans, R. (1993) *Social Auditing and Business Growth*, unpublished paper, Traidcraft, plc, Gateshead

Harrison, R. and Spoth, J. (1992) 'Matching Change Interventions to Organizational Realities', *Industrial and Commercial Training*, 24 (2)

Hawken, P. (1993) *The Ecology of Commerce: A declaration of sustainability*, HarperCollins Publishers, New York

Hopkins, D. and Leask, M. (1989) 'Performance indicators and school of development', *School Organization* 9(1), pp. 3–10

Kanter, R. M. (July/August 1994) 'Collaborative Advantage: The art of alliances', *Harvard Business Review*, 72 (4)

Kaplan, R. S. and Norton, D. P. (January/February 1992) 'The Balanced Scorecard: Measures that drive performance', *Harvard Business Review*, 70 (1), pp. 71–9

Kaplan, R. S. and Norton, D. P. (September/October1993) 'Putting the Balanced Scorecard to Work', *Harvard Business Review*, 71 (5), pp.134–47

Lloyd, T. (1990) *The Nice Company: Why nice companies make more profits*, Bloomsbury, London

Morris, J. M. (1987) 'Good Company', *Management Education and Development*, 18 (2), pp. 103–15

Palmer, C. (1994) 'The Equitable Company' in Boot, *et al.* (Eds) *Managing the Unknown: By creating new futures*, McGraw-Hill, Maidenhead

Pedler, M. J., Burgoyne, J. G. and Boydell, T. H. (1991) *The Learning*

Company: A strategy for sustainable development, McGraw-Hill, Maidenhead

Revans, R. W. (1983) *The ABC of Action Learning*, Chartwell-Bratt, Bromley

Solomon, R. (1993) *Ethics and Excellence: Cooperation and integrity in business*, Oxford University Press, Oxford

Tyneside Training and Enterprise Council (April 1994) *Traidcraft PLC and Traidcraft Exchange: Present state analysis against investors in people*, Confidential Report, Gateshead

Zadek, S. and Evans, R. (1993) *Auditing the market: A practical approach to social auditing*, Traidcraft Exchange with New Economics Foundation, Gateshead

9   Composing the company

This book began with fragmentation and ends with composition. 'Composing a Life' is the phrase used by Catherine Bateson to describe the way women make sense of their often fluid and discontinuous biographies:

> we are engaged in a day-to-day process of self-invention—not discovery, for what we search for does not exist until we find it—both the past and the future are raw material, shaped and reshaped by each individual.
>
> (1990, p. 28)

As fluidity, flux and discontinuity increasingly characterize organizations, society and our own lives, the ability to compose these things becomes more important. Reshaping what is happening via imaginative compositions that create coherence and new meanings helps to create a sense of purpose for the future.

This chapter starts with a summary of the perspective taken in this book on managing and organizing, which argues for particularism to support generative theory and organizational learning. The current passion for change and its unintended consequences are then examined, supporting the call for a theory of learning that acknowledges the part defences and resistance play in this process. Finally, we turn to speculation in composing the company that offers the hope of a new form of integration within the wider society.

Organizing for learning

Despite the ready acknowledgement of the uncertainties faced by organizations and individuals, this is an optimistic book. Learning is normal in human beings, despite the many barriers. The examples here are deliberately *ordinary*—not moments of titanic struggle, but of people going about their normal business. Yet, the individuals and organizations who are the characters in these stories show high aspirations; all set out deliberately to learn.

This book has looked at organizational learning in five sectors of the economy, but there are many other possibilities for classifying organizations. The movement from the concept of organizations as separate 'bounded entities' towards organizing as a process of service delivery and adding value, means that existing categories will break up and meld in different ways.

We take a broadly social constructionist view of the world, namely that whatever the 'objective' world may be, it is always experienced by people each in their own particular way. Thus, individuals play a very active part in interpreting, constructing and enacting the world as they see it (Berger and Luckman, 1967; Gergen, 1991). In companies and other communities, there is also a collaborative and collective construction in daily practice. Companies can be seen as 'thought collectives' and 'communities of practice' (Lave, 1991).

The approaches to knowing and learning that fit this perspective best are those that emphasize the critical role of the participants in making sense of their own experience and taking responsibility for their own actions. These are the traditions of 'action research' (Lewin, 1951), 'action science' (Argyris, *et al.*, 1985) and 'action learning' (Revans, 1979), which tend towards *grounded* rather than *grand* theory, where understanding and action is grounded in the explanations, ideas and theories of participants (Glaser and Strauss, 1967).

Against universalism

All people of broad, strong sense have an instinctive repugnance to the men of maxims because such people early discern that the mysterious complexity of our life is not to be embraced by maxims and that to lace ourselves up with formulas of that sort is to repress all the divine promptings and inspirations that spring from growing insight and sympathy. And the man of maxims is the popular representative of the minds that are guided in their moral judgement solely by general rules, thinking that this will lead them to justice by a ready-made patent method, without the trouble of exerting patience, discrimination, impartiality, without any care to assure themselves whether they have the insight that comes from a hardly earned estimate of temptation or from a life vivid and intense enough to have created a wide fellow feeling with all that is human.

(George Eliot, *The Mill on the Floss*, 1994, p. 510)

The 'men of maxims' are even more in evidence today,

especially in matters of managing and organizing. The popularity of universal, generic ideas—those that are seen as widely applicable whoever the characters, the context, the organizational setting—can limit organizational learning. Beyond universalisms, this book seeks variety and variability and celebrates the particular.

Universal management principles derive from particular settings—from the church, the army, family-owned businesses in nineteenth-century Germany and, more recently, from large capitalist enterprises in the USA and Japan. The tendency to assume their applicability in all situations requiring management or organization has greater effects with the growing social, economic and political importance of work organizations and, indeed, with the growth of formal management education. Generic notions of marketing, 'free markets', performance-related pay systems and so on are applied to industry, public services, the voluntary sector and poor agricultural societies in Africa as if all these contexts were the same. Current universal theories of management tend to be economistic, rationalistic and generic.

Economistic because they assume that organizations are market-driven, with economic efficiency being the criterion of success. The goals are sales growth, productivity, profitablity, market share, product innovations, success in the market—nothing else. In identifying nine objections to the 'unicorn of pure profit', Hampden Turner calls attention to the limitations of this approach even for the commercial sector (Hampden-Turner, 1990, pp. 222–41).

Rationalistic because, following the classical principles of Fayol (1916), Urwick (1947) and Taylor (1947), they assume that all organizations can meet their goals by means of the activities of planning, organizing, controlling, staffing and budgeting via the functions of production, finance, marketing, human resourcing. Follett (1941) was one of the few early writers who did not take this view, holding that the 'law of the situation' called for partnership, joint responsibility and multiple leadership in a democratic society. Fifty years on we are rediscovering this.

Generic because, throughout the post world war period, influential writers such as Drucker (1954), McGregor (1960), Herzberg (1968) and Mintzberg (1974), have tended to assert management as a universalistic activity. Though there is no one best way and managing does not take the same form in all organizations, nevertheless, all managers perform similar tasks and confront similar problems.

The problem with universalism is that it leads to prescription. Recently the 'TQM' and 'Excellence' movements have built on this tradition to form a new wave of generic management, providing prescriptive solutions and promising corporate success in the face of increasingly competitive global markets.

Managing is less rational, less economistic and less amenable to prescription than some of this recent wisdom implies. What 'actually happens' in most companies is much more variable, pragmatic and downright bizarre at times than we are led to believe. Furthermore such prescriptions obscure an important aspect of managerial reality. Of course issues of economic efficiency, strategy and human resources are important, of course there is much value in the ideas of TQM, excellence and 'customer service', but all these are lifeless scripts until they are acted out by a particular manager in their particular situation. Though the script be simple, performing is not.

Managing as performance art is always local, always contextual, always unrepeatable. What makes for excellence and quality here and now in one organization or at one time is often not portable. The wholesale importation of technique from one place to another is responsible for much loss of productivity and spirit. Even more seriously, it implants in the importers a persistent belief that the ideas of others are superior to their own.

For learning

In arguing this way, we soon bump up against the absurdity of fundamentalist particularism, which insists on inventing the wheels for its own cart while trying not to look at the remarkable vehicular success of a neighbour. To be able to compare and contrast—one of the fundamentals of learning—both the particular and the ability to generalize are needed. Behind the argument for particularism is the spirit of learning. Benchmarking and cherrypicking are part of the order of the day, but only as part of active experiment and the conscious learning process.

Although each seeks to address the general theme of organizational learning, the range of organizational settings in this book displays the uniqueness and idiosyncracy of company biographies and stories. Perhaps the distinction is that it is possible to *generalize about organizational learning, but that the learning company must remain a particular vision*—to be realized in the context of a unique organization with its own continuing story.

Are we learning or just changing?

Why organizational change programmes fail

Chris Argyris (1990, pp. 3 and 4) describes a study by Beer, Eisenstat and Spector (1988) in which six large companies invested heavily in change programmes to make them more competitive. The authors report that the programmes failed, either wholly or partly. They began with a big fanfare and then, like old soldiers, faded away.

The companies embarked on the change programmes because of the many poor practices they had developed that were damaging to their competitiveness. These included:

- inflexible and unadaptive rules
- managers and workers who were out of touch with customers' needs
- managers who were not committed, not cooperative and not competent to produce change
- poor interaction among functional groups
- top management refusing to believe that lower revenues and market share were more than a temporary perturbation
- lack of strategic thinking
- lower-level employees not fully informed
- low levels of trust.

Argyris asks a series of telling questions and offers some revealing answers.

Q Why is it that well-educated and well-intentioned managers, at all levels, produced these policies and practices in the first place?
A ?
Q Why did the change programmes intended to make the companies more competitive either fail or have very limited effect?
A Because most of the programmes were prepackaged, off-the-shelf products designed to be a quick success and not intimately connected with what was going on in the organization.
Q Why were such programmes selected in the first place?
A (i) Because companies emulated the programmes other companies used, and (ii) they were easy to sell to line management because they promised immediate results that top management would applaud.

However, the enthusiasm for change programmes appears to continue indiscriminately. Such recently heard comments as:

We will drive the strategy into the guts of the organization.

My staff must be made to own these changes.

It was only after we had wiped that layer of middle management that we began to realize just what it was that they did.

They constantly change what they call the strategic vision but

> they seem to have no idea this just feels like chaos at the operational level.

reveal the extent to which managers are still wedded to change practices that do not bring about the desired results. Such practices call forth the ingenuity of the resistors:

> Human beings ... show remarkable ingenuity for self-protection. They can create individual and organizational defences that are powerful and in which that power is largely in the service of the poor to mediocre performance as well as of anti-learning.
>
> (Argyris, 1990, p. 157)

The negative consequences of such actions build gradually like environmental pollution. Slowed and rendered more invisible by efforts at continuous improvement and single-loop learning, they are also covered up by daily 'defensive routines':

> The result of these countless everyday actions is to deaden individuals' awareness to the ethical pollution they are generating. My generation never realized that we were contributing to the pollution with the gas guzzlers we drove. Once we saw and understood it, we cooperated to change our actions .... It makes little sense to enact laws and rules against organizational defensive routines ... The equivalents of such laws are already in place and they do not work. The answer, as in the case of prohibition, lies in each one of us becoming self-managing and helping to create organizations that reward such self-responsible action.
>
> (Argyris, 1990, p. 161)

Yet, defences are part of self-managing. In his classic paper 'Defences and the Need to Know', Harrison shows that 'defensive behaviour' helps us adapt to a changing world. Without some certainty and stability in our lives, we cannot function. The child who continuously asks 'Why?' and who rushes from activity to activity is the same child who protests loudly when you change the words or skip a picture in a story. Our defence mechanisms are part of who we are, they help us to compose and to conduct our lives. Seeking to destroy them does not make us more effective:

> To put it strongly, the destruction of defences does not serve learning; instead it increases anxiety that we will lose the more or less effective conceptual systems with which we understand and relate to the world and we then drop back to an even more desperate and perhaps unrealistic defence than the one destroyed. Though it may seem paradoxical, we cannot increase learning by destroying the defences that block it.
>
> (Harrison, 1995, p. 290)

In the light of this, what are we to make of the notion 'resistance to change'—something all 'change agents' seek to overcome? Is it a safety net or obstacle, virtue or vice?

Freud's view was that anxiety often leads to the 'defence mechanisms' of denial, rationalisation, projection and displacement rather than to openness and learning. Beckhard's 'change equation'—D + V + M > P (where the amount of D—current dissatisfaction—plus the desirability of V—vision or model of the future—plus the quality of M—method or process for getting there—must be greater than P—the pain and cost of change for those concerned)—is all too often forgotten.

Change is not necessarily stressful of itself. Stress levels are probably far higher among the un- or underemployed than among those in demanding jobs, as long as those jobs are rewarding. Seeing stress as an inevitable consequence of change can mean that the inappropriateness, or downright silliness, of a particular development is ignored. Constant change (instability, frenzy, hyperactivity) is as harmful as overstability (rigidity, 'stuckness', agoraphobia).

Six unintended consequences of change

As well as not achieving all that is desired, the passion for organizational change in response to turbulent environments has a number of unintended consequences. These appear as imbalances and include :

- cultural crusades
- king customer
- organizational memory loss
- fear, anxiety and distrust
- organizational anorexia
- community impoverishment.

Cultural crusades

The feeling that organizations must do something every few years to keep ahead of the game fuels a fashion for successive cultural crusades. The discovery that changing the organizational structure has little real impact on its own has led to increasing interest in 'changing the culture'. Cultural change may be desirable, but not like this:

> In the face of sagging fortunes, companies become notably more willing to experiment with new ideas. It might even be argued that an indicator of managerial panic is consumption rate and shelf-life of business fads. Over two dozen managerial techniques have waxed and waned since the 1950s. More interestingly, half were spawned in the past five years. The list reads like a *Who's*

Who of business hype: Theory Z, Matrix, Managerial Grid, T groups, Intrapreneurship, Demassing, and One-Minute Managing.'

(Pascale, 1991, p. 18)

And this list is dated. How many new initiatives have touched you since 1991?

King Customer

Putting customers, clients, or users first is perhaps the most all-pervasive change in all types of organization during the last few years. This corrects an important imbalance, particularly where producers have been preoccupied with meeting their own needs. However, as we glimpsed in several chapters, customers are but one of the groups with a stake in the organization. G. Egan (1993) puts the balancing of the stakeholders at the centre of his model of effective management (see Figure 9.1).

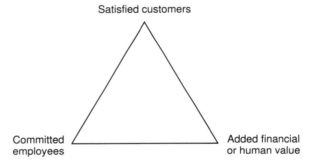

Figure 9.1   Egan's stakeholders

Unfettered customer 'rights' without responsibilities lead to breakdown. On Christmas Day 1994, as part of a sales promotion, Mercury Communications offered new customers free telephone calls to anywhere in the world. However, the lines were constantly engaged and most of these new customers could not make their calls, because a small number of about 20 callers made unbroken 12-hour international phone calls and a similar number made almost continuous shorter calls. While the company deserves some of the widespread criticism of this debacle for making promises it couldn't keep, what of those who hogged the lines because they were 'free'?

As Bateson foresaw, whenever an organism behaves as if it is the unit of survival, the result is the destruction of the environment—in this case, the telecommunications environment.

Organizational memory loss

This happens at both ends. Increases in early retirements and the removal of all those seen as clinging to old ways can have dramatic consequences. In making changes to its senior management team, an NHS Trust very quickly lost 100 years' experience of running the hospital and was left with a total of less than 5 years' experience at the top. At the other end of the age scale, young, successful managers tend to make career moves ever more quickly. Moving after a year or 18 months in post is no longer unusual. In one students' union, no officer had ever served for more than two years, so this was the extent of the organizational memory. One European-based multinational has become so concerned by this phenomenon that it has instituted a 'length of stay in job' project.

Fear, anxiety and distrust

The best companies house committed professionals willing to volunteer beyond the call of duty. However, commitment is a two-way street—unless the company gives it, it won't get it. How committed are those who are anxious and insecure for their futures, or who are angry over the fate of colleagues or over actions taken by the company in the name of all who work there?

> In one multinational corporation I worked for recently I was told that there existed within it a clandestine network that worked to prevent the company from masking some of its worst abuses to the environment and the public. They had 'leaked' information to the press and, as a result, in one instance, the company had been forced to admit liability and spend a considerable amount of money rectifying the damage that had been caused.
>
> (Charles, 1994, p. 144)

Few chief executives and top managers receive honest feedback on their decisions, recalling Joseph Heller's nightmare scenario in *Something Happened*:

> In the office in which I work there are five people of whom I am afraid. Each of these five people is afraid of four people (excluding overlaps), for a total of twenty, and each of these twenty people is afraid of six people, making a total of one hundred and twenty people who are feared by at least one person. Each of these one hundred and twenty people is afraid of the other one hundred and nineteen, and all of these one hundred and forty-five people are afraid of the twelve men at the top who helped found and build the company and now own and direct it.
>
> (1975, p. 19)

Except, of course, that if Heller were writing for the 1990s, there wouldn't be so many people in the company. The fashion for organizational anorexia helps further in creating climates of fear rather than of boldness and initiative.

Organizational anorexia

Reducing the workforce is a quick and easy route to increased 'productivity'. Many companies describe themselves as leaner and fitter as a result. However, recent evidence suggests that even the survivors of the trimming are more insecure, less trusting and less committed to their workplaces as a consequence. The effect on the wider society is even more serious.

Community impoverishment

Changes in individual organizations collectively impact on the wider society. A holidaymaker describes a journey from Italy to the UK by train:

> All the trains we travelled on were very efficient, well-maintained, arriving and leaving on time. But everywhere we went we realized how few people are now employed on the railways. In Milan the only way to buy a subway ticket was by machine. On the train through Switzerland one man was serving all the lunches, snacks and drinks on his own. He ran about for the whole journey. At the English Channel port there was only one person serving behind the counter in the transit lounge and the queue was so long that over half the people did not get served. The most dramatic part was when we arrived in Paris at 9.30 pm. We saw no staff at all on the railway platform but as we came out on to the street there were two young guards patrolling with dogs and marauding groups of young people just hanging about with nothing to do and looking rather menacing. We felt lucky just to get a taxi and leave.

Lean and fit these organizations may be, but at what cost? A professional working in a large organization comments:

> I was sympathizing with a friend, who is disappointed and frustrated that she can't get a job even after improving her qualifications, when another friend passed by. She looked terrible, absolutely exhausted. Her office has been cutting back on staff and she has so much to do.

Thus, organizations contribute to an unbalanced society, where some people struggle to cope with too much work and others atrophy for lack of it.

What is an organization that it may learn?

What can managers and other people in organizations do about this? Although much seems dictated by outside imperative, there is scope for composing companies to achieve different sorts of outcomes. The argument for focusing on learning rather than changing assumes that change is inevitable and comes whether we will it or not, but that the choice lies in our response. Acts of understanding are one alternative to the 'change programme' syndrome where, rather than demonstrating decisiveness and control, we seek to learn our way through:

> How can I decide which way to go if I don't know which way I'm facing?
>
> (John Lennon, quoted in Boot *et al.*, 1994)

An emphasis on *thinking* (Mitroff and Linstone, 1993), *seeing* (Mintzberg, 1994) and *imagination* (Morgan, 1993) characterize recent discussions of strategy. Scenario development, pioneered by Shell as far back as the 1970s, is one way of rethinking the organization and how it might change itself in the face of alternative futures. The emphasis is on freeing thinking from old patterns and imperatives so that we can see what is happening and what is possible. Ideally, there is no need for 'change programmes' in the learning company, where people take appropriate action as part of their learning/working.

How can we see or think or imagine the learning company that enriches rather than impoverishes its environment? How can we organize so that it helps us learn better, individually and together?

> There is something paradoxical here. Organizations are not merely collections of individuals, yet there is no organization without such collections. Similarly, organizational learning is not merely individual learning, yet organizations learn only through the experience and actions of individuals. What, then, are we to make of organizational learning? What is an organization that it may learn?
>
> (Argyris and Schon, 1978, pp. 9 and 10)

Thanks to people like Argyris and Schon, there is now a greater freedom of thought about the possible forms of organizing. Deming's supply chain flows horizontally through a chain of suppliers and customers (1988), and Morgan describes a general shift from 'bureaucracies to networks' (1989, p. 66). Pedler, Burgoyne and Boydell suggest that any organization must balance four functions: collective *policy* (P) and *operations* (O) and individual *action* (A) and *ideas*

(I) (1991, pp. 29–33). This 'energy flow' model (which first appeared in Chapter 4) also has four flows of energy, information and learning, represented by the four double feedback loops (shown in Figure 9.2):

policy (P) ⇔ *operations* (O) = directing
operations (O) ⇔ *action* (A) = managing
action (A) ⇔ *ideas* (I) = learning
ideas (I) ⇔ *policy* (P) = participating

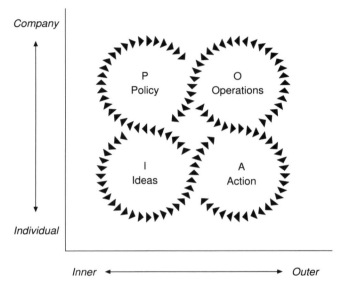

Figure 9.2 The E-Flow model of the learning company
(*Source:* Pedler, Burgoyne and Boydell, 1991, p. 32)

Philip Angier, Managing Director of Traidcraft plc, describes the way in which these flows interact in his company:

> Recently we would have been talked about internally as a command organization ... there was a clear policy framework from which we worked, we were trying to work out what that meant in terms of operational plans, then trying to communicate those down to people ...
>
> My perception would be that the policy formation was very tightly held by the Board who were trying to do a lot of listening and learning, revisiting foundation principles, working out what it meant to operate within an ethical framework, how we develop Fair Trade policies, how we apply best management practices in different directions ... but I doubt that many of the staff, or many of the representatives and customers and all the people we are

now calling stakeholders, felt that they had a way of influencing the organization. The policy formation province was the Board and the trustees and other policy formers talking amongst themselves and to other outside peer groups ...

Transparency and openness is an important aspect of our social accounting process and it causes you to lay out the issues in the open for *everyone* to see ... we're opening ourselves up and that's very much part of an organizational learning process—whether it's the press or a producer partner or another stakeholder, people can feed back and we can learn from that.

Chris Bones, personnel director with United Distillers, describes the development and implementation of a worldwide climate survey:

We've had the *idea*, which is to have the survey, we're pretty clearly structured with some *policy* overview and I guess what I'm really trying to drive through now is how do you put that in *operation*. Of course that in itself requires new ideas, new policies and individual *actions*. But yesterday's meeting with the task force was all very operational ... I now have to go away and be all operational for a bit. (Added emphasis)

Big companies, like small ones, differ widely in character. In United Distillers, there is a whole range of policy inputs—group policies from Guinness, company ones from the executive, broad personnel principles from that function and individual regional policies from around the world.

Ideas, Policy, Operations and Action in United Distillers

Policy starts with the ideas of individuals who get them cleared at higher levels:

there's an interactive process ... I have to check that what we're going to do—how we're going to handle it—that it doesn't contravene anything the Group feels is important or which would affect Guinness' reputation in the wider arena ... stakeholder relations, financial institutions or whatever, so that if someone got hold of it and published it, we wouldn't be embarrassed .... It's our 'honest, legal and decent checklist'.

The process is quite informal and emerges from interaction and relationships:

... broad-brush Group policies will quite often come verbally ... or from individuals. We have invited the Group PR Manager onto our task force so it will come from her as the holder of 'Group guidance'. The executive policy will be written to some extent ... I did a paper following an objectives review for the project by the MD and the Personnel Director and based on a meeting with colleagues to give me ideas and general guidance ... then I cleared the paper through the Regional Personnel team and then the UD Personnel Director takes it to the exec.

It's a good example of how UD works ... there's a lot of informal communication so it's a matter of skill in managing the project to make sure enough people get on board on a relationship basis. There's no written-down process—unlike Shell, where I used to work, where you consult the following in the following order. It's very much driven by your intuition and understanding of how things should work ....

The directors 'sign off' rather than initiate policy:

... something like over 90 per cent of the decisions involving policy are made outside the boardroom ... therefore, as managers, individually we have an immense amount of influence on the direction the business takes. Something like this survey which will hit every single one of our 12 000 employees worldwide ... has been very considerably influenced by 4 people.

Then the person championing the idea becomes the operations manager:

Especially in our business, which is a sort of federated business, you have to create ownership for policy, you can't impose it ... whereas maybe in the Health Service things are more directive—'this is now the policy'. It's a rolling consultative process and the best way to do this is with a task force which has most of the vested interests represented in it. At times we are faced with senior people's agendas and have to see how these fit into those of regional markets. Can we make that work? So we've had 5 drafts, which I sent out each time, and people go away and talk to all sorts of people, and I've just about managed to take 90 per cent of what everybody said ... so we now have a pilot which is acceptable to the world—quite an achievement really.

The flow from policy to operations to the ideas—of *all* the people involved—is a collective meaning-making process, that creates a flow of ownership essential for collaborative action:

So there's a lot about making people feel comfortable, making them feel listened to, understood and that somehow their needs are being reflected in the outcome ... so that's how you make meaning ... you turn it into ownership—meaning means developing ownership.

As these accounts illustrate, the patterns and flows of ideas, policies, operations and actions differ between particular companies. Using four pictures, we can imagine a progression from the simpler 'command and control' to the more complex 'networking' organization, showing how the four functions change in their relationship with the differently composed companies.

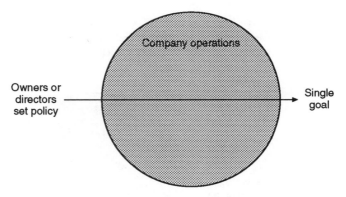

Figure 9.3 *The* controlled *company (P→O→A; No I)*

In the controlled company (see Figure 9.3), there is a top-down prescription of policy (P), translated into an operations plan (O), which is managed into action (A). Ideas (I) do not figure as there is little interest in the ideas of the people in the company as a whole, just in those generated at the top to form the policies in the first place.

In the *participative* company (see Figure 9.4), there is more involvement of other people's ideas.

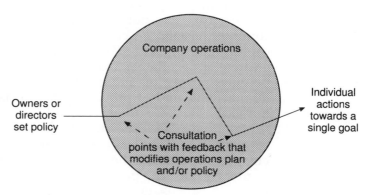

Figure 9.4 *The* participative *company (P→O→A + I)*

Here, things are still pretty much hierarchical and people know their places, but attempts are made to consult and gather suggestions from people in the company. This allows for course corrections on the basis of feedback and new information and, hence, a somewhat more flexible, emergent strategy. There remains a clear and single direction and path to the goal, as set by those at the top.

In the *empowered* company (see Figure 9.5), those senior people find it hard to set a single direction and offer, instead, a broad set of values, vision, purpose and mission.

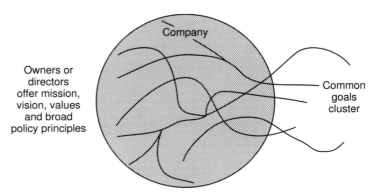

Owners or directors offer mission, vision, values and broad policy principles

Common goals cluster

Company

Figure 9.5   The empowered *company (P→I→A + 0)*

This results in a number of different paths being taken by individuals and project teams towards the common vision, some of which merge and split at various points. Project leaders, operations directors and information technologists work at mapping, coordination and coherence. Rather than a single goal, the output is a goals cluster realizing the common vision. *Policy* is now aimed at engaging *ideas*, capturing hearts and minds, in the belief that this will lead to creative *action*. Rather than preceding *action*, *operations* now becomes a way of understanding and coordinating individual actions, and of providing the crucial feedback function to *policy*.

Many creative concerns, such as software companies, bespoke manufacturers, professional practices and consultancy firms resemble the empowered company more than the command one. The professional parts of some organizations, such as hospitals, universities, R&D companies, where individuals exercise a great deal of self-management and autonomy, also fit this pattern.

In Figure 9.6, the organization is composed in a way that is more and more integrated with its surrounding communities and environments, linking inside and outside on projects and processes.

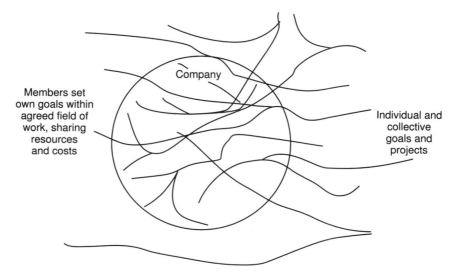

Members set
own goals within
agreed field of
work, sharing
resources
and costs

Company

Individual and
collective
goals and
projects

Figure 9.6 The consortium *company (I+O+[O+P])*

In the network, federation or consortium, *ideas* and *action* have clear precedence as members pursue their own ideas, projects and practices. *Operations* and *policy* are less in evidence, but, paradoxically, require frequent discussion and negotiation. This organization model may be most user-friendly—the fastest of all in response to users or customers. For it to work at all, members must be highly motivated, independent, energetic and proactive. They may work together collaboratively—sometimes in regular partnerships, sometimes as jobs demand—and there is much interaction with people outside the company. People tend to cover their own costs, paying a tithe to support shared services. This model may be less stable than previous ones, with old members leaving and new ones joining, and also in terms of the whole organization dissolving and re-forming from time to time.

These pictures illustrate some possibilities for composing organizations for learning with variations on the themes of policy, operations, ideas and action. The move towards the more 'virtual', networked, consortium form of company brings with it the ability to create internal conditions for participation, collective meaning-making and ownership. This form, with its porousness, openness, boundarylessness and responsiveness, offers opportunities for the reintegration of the company with its external environment.

Learning in your company

How you respond to these pictures is up to you. Morgan's eight images of organization liberate us from any one model; we can have as many, or as few, views of our company as we can cope with (1986). The rich variety of even the small number of organizations visited in this book goes well beyond any single image of 'learning company'.

At the outset, we attempted a classification of company types and chapters by complexity and purpose. This works only as a sandcastle works—until the next wave. We hope that the ideas in this book will be generative; different bits may be more applicable to certain kinds of companies because of the particular problems and dilemmas they share—lifecycle biography in the small firm, developing organizational memory and company-wide learning in the large, learning from professional accountability in public services and so on. However, such themes as:

- fragmentation, chaos and learning
- linking individual and organizational learning
- the company as a developing being
- future skills (looking forward)
- organizational memory (looking back)
- learning for professional accountability
- managing with volunteers
- participation in policy making
- the balanced scorecard—learning and its consequences
- composing the company

have some relevance in most organizations. In any particular company, generating ideas for organizational learning means interpreting, translating and reinventing these common themes. Most generalizable of all is the learning process itself. If there is one single lesson from these examples of organizational learning in practice, it is that companies can organize in ways that make learning more or less possible. Learning how to learn has become inseparable from learning how to manage. Some points about this learning process are that:

- a company may be able to study and become aware of its learning processes and habits and improve on them
- we learn in companies from the *problems, dilemmas* or *difficulties* we encounter, together with our attempts to overcome them
- these problems, dilemmas or difficulties are, in some ways, unique to our company—we have to take charge of our own learning and not rely wholly on the 'wisdom' of benchmarking, management gurus or any other external source

- what a company learns depends on the problems or issues it faces now, and its long-term success and survival depends upon its ability to do this repeatedly and appropriately. It can therefore *choose* problems to learn from; that is, it can be pro-active, and not just responsive or adaptive in reaction
- from time to time the problem a company is facing may be so important that it causes us to look very seriously at our basic assumptions and ways of doing business. Learning in this context is not incremental or improving but discontinuous and *transformational*, that is, it changes us in some fundamental way.

Towards a learning society

The last issue in this book is a transformation hardly yet dreamed of: the part that organizations might play in creating a learning society. At this point, it is appropriate to remind ourselves that we have not always been so here-and-now-focused:

> ... there are native American people who, when making decisions, consider the effect that their actions will have on seven generations to come.
>
> (Charles, 1994, p. 142)

Such a time frame is almost inconceivable to the peoples of the 'nanosecond nineties', yet many of the children born now can expect to be alive in 2070. What sort of a world are our learning organizations helping to create for them? In his sobering evidence of the effects of recent changes in the UK, Hutton describes the effects on income distribution:

> If the population of Britain were divided according to income, if income were made equivalent to height and if the population then marched past for an hour, it would take a full 37 minutes before the first adult of average height was seen. For the first 15 minutes there would be a parade of dwarves. Stature would increase gradually thereafter, but 57 minutes would have to pass before we saw people of twice the average height. Giants of 90 feet or more would appear in the last few seconds, with the last one or two literally miles high.
>
> (1995, p. 193)

At what time would *you* be walking past?

And where would your friends come? (Fairly close to you?) Where will your children come?

And, what connection do you have with people half an hour away from you?

This is the 30:30:40 society. The first 30 per cent are the

disadvantaged—unemployed or economically inactive; the second 30 per cent are the *marginalized* and *insecure*—working part time, on short contracts, casually or with no formal employment protection; only 40 per cent are employed full time, on permanent contracts or in established self-employment. These are the *privileged*, even though 35 per cent of them earn less than 80 per cent of the median (Hutton, 1995 pp. 106–8).

This book, like most in the field, dwells mainly on the privileged 40 per cent. In an era that has seen the Welfare State ethos challenged and eroded and with it the responsibility of the State for the health, education and training of all its citizens, work organizations stand out more strongly as accumulators and distributors of wealth, power and opportunity. Those inside organizations on a permanent, well-paid and 'full benefits' basis, are, increasingly, in a minority; those outside organizations or who are minimally and temporarily attached are the majority.

One scenario sees organizations becoming more learningful, also more successful and, at the same time, smaller, more exclusive, more isolated from those who have not. Yet, wide inequalities tend to make for instability, both economically and socially. Connecting with those outside the organization is thus important for the long-term survival of any company.

It is imperative to remember that the same energy and learning potential that exists in people inside organizations is also to be found in those outside. This may be temporarily masked by disappointment and a sense of rejection, but it is seldom entirely destroyed. In learning about organizational learning, we note that a learning organization seeks to enhance and harness the learning potential of all its members—we need *all* the available intelligence, ingenuity and commitment, and not just that of the few at the apex. This much is rapidly becoming orthodoxy, but what of the 60 per cent outside organizations? They, too, have the potential for learning and for making a contribution. Tapping this potential energy can surprise, as shown by the Manor Employment Project (MEP).

CASE: The Manor Employment Project

The MEP was established in 1980 as an employment creation initiative on the Lower Manor housing estate in Sheffield. With the aid of local authority grants and in partnership with various professionals from the better-off western half of the city, Manor residents set about creating jobs and businesses on a derelict four-acre site. The MEP was a response to the tide of unemployment and poverty, which rose dramatically after 1979, exacerbated by the decline of the local steel industry. In 1984, of the 220 school-leavers from the local Waltheof School, only 19 found employment.

It was easy to romanticize MEP, with its cooperatives, community governance and heroic tales of development—of both individuals and of businesses, several of which continue to exist in the city today. At its peak, MEP had 50 people working in businesses such as Silver Needles (fashion wear), Procon (concrete pavings) and Prince Car Valeting, with a collective turnover of some £250 000. After five years and several attempts, MEP was externally evaluated by City Council officers. By then, it had received about £150 000 in grant aid, some of which paid for five staff, as well as the rent and rates-free site, and many of the jobs it had created in the then 10 businesses were poorly paid and part time. (By comparison, we can note that permanant jobs created in the Spanish Mondragon cooperatives—an early model for the MEP's pioneers—were costed at £35 000 each—a not dissimilar figure to that for many of the more recent UK urban development corporations.)

The Council review was not able to quantify many of the spin-off benefits of MEP, such as the Manor Mercury (a newspaper), the Manor Nursery and a Wildlife Scheme, which eventually employed more than 50 people. Nor did it take much account of the less tangible, but important, educational and social value of the MEP. From the beginning, the driving energy for the project as a whole lay with the women, while men concentrated more single-mindedly on business. Gender issues were often as important as business ones—a failure in terms of a purely business-based evaluation (and therefore, in terms of MEP's stated objectives, of job creation), but quite a different matter in terms of cultural, social and community development.

On reflection, MEP's Development Worker, Dave Clarson, notes:

> ... perhaps it was about giving people the opportunity to make choices for themselves ... you could say all these people are unemployed, they're not going to get a job anywhere ... I don't know whether it was much to do with whether the business would be a success particularly or whether it was more to do with giving the individuals involved an opportunity to be positive, to do different things, to experiment ...

But you can't support these things with business development funding. The effect of the Council's evaluation was an orderly winding up of MEP over the next 18 months, but also in its reincarnation as The Manor Training and Resources Centre (MaTReC) in 1987. MaTReC continues with great success and increased funding today, its strength and vitality, in part, a legacy from the endeavours, struggles and achievements of the MEP. (Based on Pedler *et al.* 1990)

What does this mean for existing organizations? Some, most obviously but not exclusively in the voluntary sector, are closely linked with those outside the formal economy. For others, the link may be less clear. Some argue that business and financial leaders are unable to take on the problems of environmental sustainability, worldwide poverty, unemployment and ill health:

> To accept responsibility for them would mean redefining business goals and business success .... Their overriding priority must be to survive and succeed in today's corporate jungle.
>
> (Robertson, 1995, p. 160)

Robertson does not see a solution coming from within any existing organizations, but thinks that only independent citizens and independent movements are free to map out a route to a new future. Yet, the apparently taken-for-granted late twentieth-century focus on survival, competition and profit may be something of an aberration. Solomon points out that the profit motive alone is not an adequate justification for action. We do not talk about a 'rent motive' or 'a wage motive' and 'I'm sorry, your Honour, I just had this overwhelming murder motive' would cut little ice in a court of law (1993, p. 40). Profit as the be-all and end-all is:

> ... a serious obstacle to understanding the rich tapestry of motives and actions that make up the business world.
>
> [the] unsung history of business [is its contribution to a prosperous society and] the traditional virtues of responsibility, community and integrity.
>
> (Solomon, 1993, pp. 47 and 17)

and a source of personal disaster, as Erich Fromm pointed out years ago:

> Many a businessman feels himself the prisoner of his business and the commodities he sells; he has a feeling of fraudulency about his product and a secret contempt for it. He hates his competitors because they are a threat; his employees as well as his superiors, because he is in a constant competitive fight with them. Most important of all, he hates himself, because he sees his life passing by, without making any sense beyond the momentary intoxication of success.
>
> (1941, p. 9)

In the public sector, where institutions attempt to separate their governance from their constituent communities, things can go badly wrong. Some higher education institutions have recently cast students, not as junior members of the academic community, but as consumers, able to take or leave their education but with no right to representation on the board. Wagner sees staff and students as '... the real capital stock ... and the key to the intellectual health' of such institutions and suggests that they must be partners in the governance of their communities (in Farnham and Horton, 1992, p. 240). Anthropologist Jane Jacobs has warned of the dangers in confusing two quite different 'moral syndromes', those of the 'Guardian' and the 'Commercial'. She warns that, because they are separate and each is internally coherent, you must live by all of the precepts. Borrowing bits from each does not lead to a productive synthesis but to 'monstrous hybrids' or 'systematic moral corruption' (Jacobs, 1992).

Nevertheless, perhaps we are reaching the end of the period when we have sought balance in society by having the public services and the voluntary organizations deal with the problems that are not the business of business. Leaving it to pressure groups to change things by boycotting certain products or protesting against particular activities seems suddenly inadequate. Boundaries and definitions are loosening in an era of uncertainty, and also of individuality in which we each take more personal responsibility for our actions in the wider context.

Consider the perspective you take when deciding how to act:

Application 17: Your perspective for action

The world/humanity	**The world/humanity**
The country	**The country**
The local community	**The local community**
My organization	**My organization**
My department	My department
Myself/my family	Myself/my family

1. Which of these perspectives is *most* characteristic of you?

_____

2. Which are you most likely to neglect?

_____

3. What are the consequences of this for you?

_____

_____

_____

4. What might be the consequences for others?

_____

_____

_____

It's hard to hold more than one perspective in mind at a time. An organization that did this would look outside its boundaries in many different ways. It would recognize itself at all times as an organization that is part of a healthy society. If so—perhaps—a job interview of the future ... ?

Maria is 32 years old and an information technology specialist. She has always found her work compelling and consuming and, by working hard, has risen rapidly in her present company. Now running out of headroom, she is attracted by a job advertisement for Healthy Enterprise plc, a new and rapidly expanding software engineering company, which operates a network of several dozen small plants spanning the globe. The advertisement calls for 'energetic, imaginative people', but also for those who are 'self-managing, self-responsible, who operate well in partnership with others, are skilled in relational learning [what did *that* mean?] and who seek balance in their lives'. She was intrigued. She was pleased to hear that she had been shortlisted.

Now Maria was puzzled. She felt that she was presenting herself well in the interview. She had not been thrown by the wide-ranging questions. She had displayed a thorough knowledge of what would be required of her and had made very clear her past record of producing results, attention to detail, willingness to work any hours that were needed while, at the same time stressing her enthusiasm and creativity. She had already been told that her references were excellent.

Yet she was aware that the three people interviewing her were not entirely happy. One leaned forward. 'We understand that you perform very well at work and that you keep yourself fit', she said, 'but we are worried that you do not seem to have any life outside. What part do you play in your community? Do you have a family? When do you see your friends?

Maria was nonplussed. Her family lived miles away. Her two-year relationship had just broken up; there was so little time to spend together. After this, she had thrown herself even harder into work. Her interviewer continued, 'What do you do to enjoy yourself? We are a forward-thinking company, very anxious to be a part of the community and to lead balanced lives. Where is the balance in yours?'

Maria could think of nothing to say.

References

Argyris, C. (1990) *Overcoming Organizational Defences: Facilitating organizational learning,* Allyn & Bacon, Boston

Argyris, C., Putnam, R. and Smith, D. M. (1985) *Action Science: Concepts, methods and skills for research and information,* Jossey Bass, San Francisco

Argyris, C. and Schon, D. (1978) *Organizational Learning: A theory of action perspective,* Addison-Wesley, Reading, Massachusetts

Bateson, C. (1990) *Composing a Life,* Plume (Penguin Books) New York

Beer, M. Eisenstat, R. and Spector, B. (1988) *The Critical Path to Change: Developing the competitive organization,* Harvard Business School Press, Boston

Berger, P. and Luckman, T. (1966) *The Social Construction of Reality*, Penguin, Harmondsworth, Middlesex

Boot, R. L., Morris, J. M. and Lawrence, J. (Eds) (1994) *Managing the Unknown: By creating new futures*, McGraw-Hill, Maidenhead

Charles, E., 'New Futures, at Whose Cost?', in Boot, R. *et al.* (Eds) (1994) *Managing the Unknown: By creating new futures*, McGraw-Hill, Maidenhead

Deming, W. E. (1988) *Out of the Crisis*, Cambridge University Press, Cambridge

Drucker, P. (1954) *The Practice of Management*, Harper and Row, New York

Egan, G. (1993) *Adding Value: A systematic guide to business-driven management and leadership*, Jossey Bass, San Francisco

Eliot, G. (1994) *The Mill on the Floss*, Penguin, Harmondsworth, Middlesex, p. 510

Farnham, D. and Horton, S. (1993) *Managing the New Public Services*, Macmillan, London

Fayol, H. (1916) *Aministration Industrielle et Générale*, translated by Constance Storrs, (1949) Pitman, London

Follett, M. P. (1941) *Dynamic Administration*, Pitman, London

Fromm, E. (1941) *Escape from Freedom*, Farrar, Strauss and Giroux, New York.

Gergen, K. (1991) *The Saturated Self*, HarperCollins, New York.

Glaser, B. and Strauss, A. (1967) *The Discovery of Grounded Theory*, Aldine, Chicago

Harrison, R., 'Barriers to Learning in an Organization', in Boot, R. *et al.* (Eds) (1994) *Managing the Unknown: By creating new futures*, McGraw-Hill, Maidenhead

Harrison, R. (1995) *Collected Papers*, McGraw-Hill, Maidenhead

Heller, J. (1975) *Something Happened*, Corgi, London, p. 19

Herzberg, F. (January/February 1968) 'One More Time: How do you Motivate Employees?', *Harvard Business Review*, pp. 53–62

Hutton, W. (1995) *The State We're In*, Jonathan Cape, London

Jacobs, J. (1992) *Systems of Survival: A dialogue on the moral foundations of commerce and politics*, Hodder & Stoughton, London

Lave, J. (1991) 'Situating Learning in Communities of Practice', in Resnick, L. B., Levine, J. M., and Teasley, S. D. (Eds) *Perspectives in Socially Shared Cognition*, American Psychological Association, Washington DC

Lewin, K. (1951) *Field Theory in Social Science*, Harper & Row, New York

McGregor, D. (1960) *The Human Side of Enterprise*, McGraw-Hill, New York

Mintzberg, H. (1974) *The Nature of Managerial Work*, Harper & Row, New York

Mintzberg, H., 'Strategic Thinking as "Seeing"', in Garratt, R. (Ed.) (1994) *Developing Strategic Thought: Rediscovering the art of direction-giving*, McGraw-Hill, Maidenhead

Mitroff, I I. and Linstone, H. A. (1993) *The Unbounded Mind*, Oxford University Press, New York

Morgan, G. (1986) *Images of Organizations*, Sage, London

Morgan, G. (1989) *Creative Organization Theory*, Sage, London

Morgan, G. (1993) *Imaginization*, Sage, London

Pascale, R. T. (1991) *Managing on the Edge*, Penguin, Harmondsworth, Middlesex

Pedler, M. J., Banfield, P., Boraston, I., Gill, J. and Shipton, J. (1990) *The Community Development Initiative: A story of the Manor Employment Project in Sheffield*, Avebury, Gower, Aldershot

Pedler, M, J., Burgoyne, J. G. and Boydell, T. H. (1991) *The Learning Company: A strategy for sustainable development*, McGraw-Hill, Maidenhead

Revans, R. W. (1979) *Developing Effective Managers*, Praeger, New York

Robertson, J. 'Shaping the Post-modern Economy: Can Business Play a Creative Part?', in Boot, R. *et al.* (Eds) (1995) *Managing the Unknown: By creating new futures*, McGraw-Hill, Maidenhead

Soloman, R. (1992) *Ethics and Excellence: Cooperation and Integrity in Business*, Oxford University Press, Oxford

Taylor, F. W. (1947) *Scientific Management*, Harper & Row, New York

Urwick, L. F. (1947) *The Elements of Administration*, Pitman, London

INDEX